elf-study workbooks

Practical Leadership Skills

Russell Tobin

**KOGAN
PAGE**

The masculine pronoun has been used throughout this book. This stems from a desire to avoid ugly or cumbersome language, and no discrimination, prejudice or bias is intended.

First published by Fenman in 1996

Second edition published by Kogan Page in 1999

Kogan Page Limited   Stylus Publishing Inc.
120 Pentonville Road   22883 Quicksilver Drive
London N1 9JN, UK   Sterling, VA 20166, USA

British Library Cataloguing in Publication Data.
A record for this book is available from the British Library.

ISBN 0 7494 2965 8

Printed and bound in Great Britain by Biddles Ltd, Guildford and King's Lynn

TABLE OF CONTENTS

Page

Introduction

How this book can help you   1

Study methods   2

What support is available?   3

For the reader's boss   4

Good leadership: what does it look like?   6

The framework of critical skills   8

The skills in detail, with coaching questions

Skill 1, about self-esteem - for you and for them   11

Skill 2, about problems and confrontation   29

Skill 3, about assumptions and their consequences   45

Skill 4, about consultation and coaching   57

Skill 5, about responsibility and delegation   75

Skill 6, about action - and the right level of detail   87

Skill 7, about control and about learning   101

More about teams   119

- the leader's reponsibilities   120

- the members' reponsibilities   129

- team roles   131

Summary - showing the pages which your boss/coach/
tutor may want to see after completion - and,
perhaps, review again in a few weeks' time.   133

Pocket card   135

Working towards a qualification?   136

HOW THIS BOOK CAN HELP YOU

"How do I ensure that I consistently handle my people well? How do I make sure I get the best out of them? How do I get through an awkard situation without losing someone's co-operation? How do I bring together different people management theories in a meaningful way?"

As a manager (team leader, section head, co-ordinator or whatever) you know that people cannot be taken for granted. Certainly, when it comes to motivating (or de-motivating) your staff, the types of discussion shown in the diagram below will be significant.

They are the sort of deliberate, work-centred discussions which you have with your people at the workplace. They are the discussions through which, knowingly or not, you channel your own attitudes and values.

As you can see, these discussions focus on different areas, some of which may not come up too often. Fortunately, though, they share just seven common skills, the all-the-time, *practical*, leadership skills, which are the subject of this book.

Those seven skills are the foundation for the other, more targeted, work discussions, which are dealt with in dedicated books. They all demonstrate these practical leadership skills being used in a wide range of situations. This book will help you to learn these skills so that you can apply them at any time.

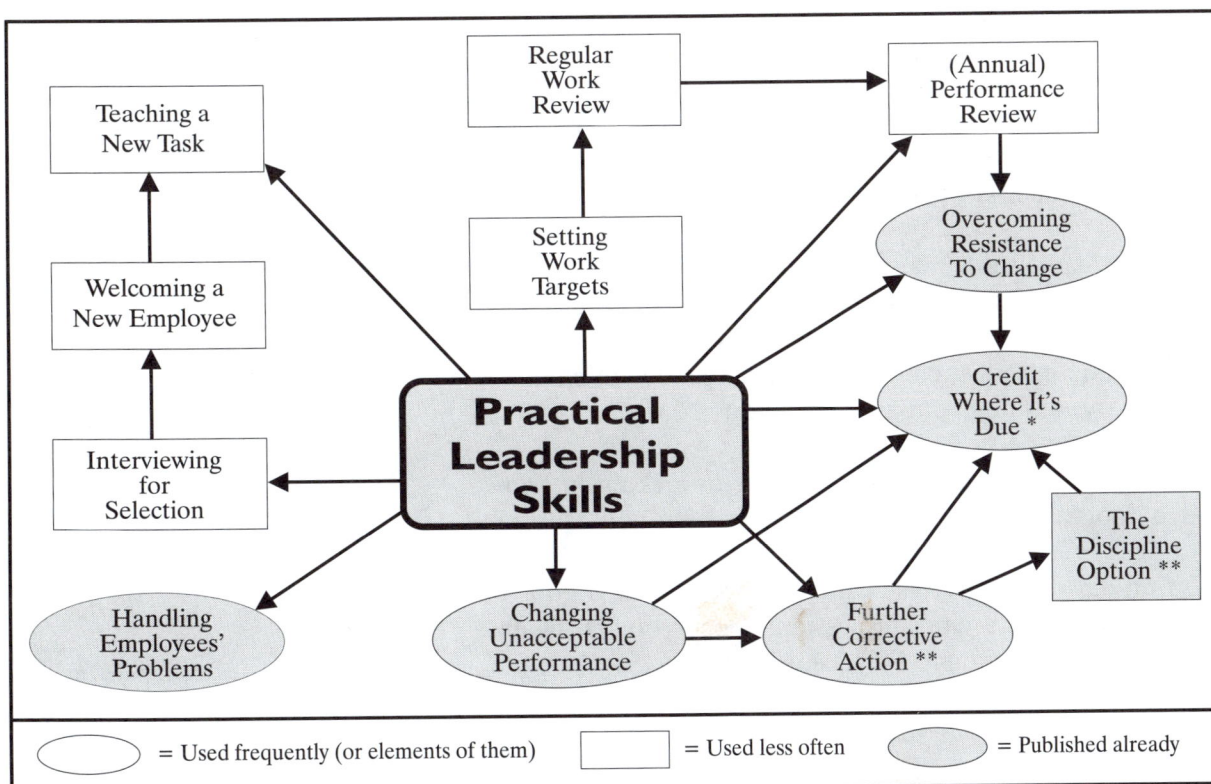

* First published as 'Recognising Dependable Work'.   ** These are combined in one book which will help to avoid claims against you.

STUDY METHODS

Nothing difficult here; there are three main study methods: reading, thinking and writing.

Thinking is the hardest part but writing your responses in the *questionnaires* will help that process.

The questionnaires are collections of coaching questions which ask you to reflect on your own experience, your own job, your own people and your own behaviour.

Think what your responses tell you about the way you handle your people and how you see them. You'll probably feel reinforced in many of the things you do but you may also feel that you could change the way you do some things.

Further questions ask you to consider what you will change back on the job. And, because changing things back on the job is what this is all about, you'll find it really useful to *write down* what you intend to do. That way you can check back later to see how well you carried out your intentions.

That makes: reading, thinking, writing and *implementation*.

Finally, having had a go at changing things (sometimes your own behaviour) you should review how well the implementation went. Do you need to do some more tweaking? Do you need to read one or more sections again? Do you need to talk things over with a colleague?

That makes: reading, thinking, writing, implementation and *review*; an important part of the *learning cycle*.

You can read all this material and complete the questionnaires - which have a picture of a pencil in the margin, as here - in two to four hours. Or you can work through this introduction and the other sections in small chunks, trying things out as it suits you.

If any questions make you feel unsure, or lacking in knowledge, look at the next page to see what help you can seek.

To find out if it really will work for you, *give it a go:* before you finish a work discussion, check yourself against these skills. Experiment. Persevere. *Get feedback.*

This grey panel is for your own notes as you work.

WHAT SUPPORT IS AVAILABLE?

Your own powers of observation provide good support. Ask yourself who are the most effective managers or team leaders you have met. Observe how they deal with their staff and other people and you will recognise that most of them do at least some of the things outlined here. If they are effective in the long term they will be doing all these things.

These skills may need hard work so don't be afraid to ask for support from the following.

YOUR BOSS   S/he wants you to succeed and may also *coach* you on your work in this module. The next page is for your boss.

COLLEAGUES   They want members of their team to be effective. They also know that if they give help to you they can request help from you later.

YOUR STAFF   They need you to be effective. And, because they see you as no one else sees you, they can give you constructive feedback. But you may need to encourage them to do so.

YOUR TUTOR   If you have a separate tutor s/he will probably be a member of the training department and they *need* you to succeed.

THE AUTHOR   If you look again at the range of discussions shown on page 1 you will see that some occur more frequently than others. For these there are further self-study modules. All help you to develop these Practical Leadership Skills in specific ways in a range of situations which are important to you and your people.

If the first three above know what you are doing - and you may need to tell them - they can help. Mutual support is good teamwork so why not enlist their support?

FOR THE READER'S BOSS

One or more of your staff, managers who report to you and who are working through this book, may be wondering just how serious you are about helping, or wanting, them to improve their skills with people.

So your visible interest is a powerful motivator for your managers and, like all coaching, it doesn't have to take much of your time. It can also be pleasurable, as you see your managers improve; and as you see this improvement contributing towards better results from your whole team.

Your help is *really important*; here are two main ways to give it.

1. Feedback on your own observations

You can observe how a manager, in a regular meeting, applies the seven skills outlined here, then give objective feedback against those skills because they are so specific.

For example, you might say to Simon, a junior manager, "I liked the way you (used Skill No. 4); did you notice the effect on Leslie?" This gets Simon thinking of the benefits of using that skill. You might then ask, "Can you recall the words you used?" This positive feedback encourages him to use that skill again.

Conversely, with negative behaviour you might ask, "Did you notice Jackie's reaction when you (said such and such)?"

Here, you'll have noticed, this feedback starts with a question. The question comes first in order to get your manager thinking.

If he had noticed Jackie's reaction that's good; it means you don't actually have to give the negative words yourself. But if he didn't notice, you can tell him. Either way you can then ask, "Which of the Practical Leadership Skills would have helped in that situation?"

You can then ask how the employee will change next time. Thus, they have *quickly* reviewed an activity in order to improve, and they have a simple plan for improvement.

2.   Coaching

Coaching by you helps to shape the employee's behaviour on the job and this book is a powerful tool for coaching. Even one section can be useful if there is something particular which a manager ought to be focusing on.

The questions on the previous page are examples of coaching questions. If you read your employee's responses to the questionnaires in this book you can ask similar questions about those responses. This lets you assess the manager's understanding and add your own guidance, perhaps in the form of more coaching questions, if you think it is needed.

Ideally you should see the managers' completed responses a few minutes before he or she comes in. At worst you can quickly scan (some of) your employee's responses when they arrive. Either way, your questions can come in three broad categories. Here are simple examples.

- Follow through.   "I see (under, eg, Skill 2) you thought there was scope for improvement with (such and such). *Have you thought how you will handle that?"*

- Checking.   "(Eg, Skill 3) seems to have got you thinking. *Could this skill have any relevance to (a problem that) you thought existed)?"*

- Exploring.   "Under (eg, Skill 5) I see you mentioned (such and such). *Can you think of any other examples (or how else this applies to your job)?"*

There is, of course, a fourth category which covers your own likes and dislikes, eg, "This bit on page 99 about (whatever). *What do you think of what they say here?"* And then you can challenge or support what the manager says. This lets you convey your own views which, we hope, will endorse what the author has said.

When you start to understand how your people think you also learn something about how far you can trust them. That has to be a good thing.

GOOD LEADERSHIP:

WHAT DOES IT LOOK LIKE?

The author has asked hundreds of managers the question,

> "How, during day-to-day discussions, does an
> effective manager gain the co-operation,
> goodwill and effectiveness of his/her staff?

Would you like to try answering that question yourself?
Take five minutes to focus on what effective managers
actually *do or say* during work-centred discussions. You
don't have to go into great detail, broad headings will do.
(You could also ask your colleagues what they think too.)

Your thoughts:

```
............................................................
............................................................
............................................................
............................................................
............................................................
............................................................
............................................................
............................................................
............................................................
............................................................
```

Comments are overleaf.

Good leadership: What does it look like?

In answering this question managers usually produce, as would most people, lists of traits, characteristics, attitudes, or generalisations. However, people infer these attitudes, etc., from what they observe about the way a person *behaves*.

They may give broad descriptions such as "communicates well", but this raises the question, "What do they do, *specifically*, that makes you say they communicate well?" Or, "Sets a good example." What are they actually *doing* that makes people say, "They set a good example"? Seldom does an item on the list describe a specific and *observable behaviour*, but *that* is what is needed.

If you know what behaviours are effective you can watch how a boss works with an employee and can say whether the boss did, or did not, use a specific behaviour. More importantly, of course, you can check if you use these behaviours yourself. You can practise using them and obtain feedback on your success.

Before you continue:

Look back to your own list; see if you can discriminate between:

- specific behaviours on the one hand (please mark them with a letter B), and

- on the other hand, generalisations, traits, attitudes, or characteristics (mark them with a G) .

Please do this now because understanding the difference is really important, and the behaviours described on the next page are deceptively simple.

By the way

Did you have a go at the task on page 6? Did you review what you wrote, as you were asked above?

If you did, fine. If you didn't, are you missing an opportunity? If you didn't take the time to write, did you take the time to think? (Just asking.)

THE FRAMEWORK OF CRITICAL SKILLS

Practical Leadership Skills are effective *behaviour.*

Descriptions of effective behaviours should provide practical guidance without being so narrow as to be restrictive, nor so vague as to be useless. The seven skills in this book are effective, *and observable*, behaviours.

They provide an approach to leadership which balances concern for the task with concern for the person. You can choose whether to use these behaviours - or not - and how to emphasise each one according to the circumstances. You can observe if you and other people are using the seven skills, as appropriate - or going against any of them.

Practical Leadership Skills

1. Maintain or enhance the self-esteem of the employee.

2. Don't attack the person,
    FOCUS ON THE PROBLEM.

3. Don't assume that the employee has committed an offence.

4. Encourage the employee to express their opinions and make suggestions.

5. Allow the employee adequate time to think through the problem and to suggest a solution.

6. Ensure that the employee has an appropriate ACTION programme.

7. Always set a specific follow-up date.

For solving problems and for creating effective working relationships, these seven skills are sound common sense (just consider the opposite of each).

They help to achieve a consistent approach to people in one-to-one situations and in larger meetings. They are also valuable for members of a team working together.

They may well confirm what you, as a manager, do already and therefore know to be right, or they may offer an *additional* way of handling people at work. You'll use most of these skills in most work-centred discussions, but not necessarily all of them; they comprise a *framework*, something which you can flesh out to suit yourself and use as you wish in the situation you are handling.

If you ever have to handle an awkward situation for which you have no specific guidelines you will find it useful to have these seven skills in mind when you prepare for the meeting. And, before you finish most work-centred discussions, you'll also find it useful to run a quick mental check against each one.

Certainly, for most people anyway, these skills are not second nature, they have to be worked at. Why they make good sense, and how you can use them, is explained in the pages that follow.

Hold on there

Did you consider the opposite of each of those seven skills?

Why not take a couple of minutes to note the opposites in the grey panel opposite the skills. Or list them below; just as you wish. Because, when you recognise the opposites it's nice to have the antidote to hand, so to speak.

Ask yourself this

Depending on the reading you've done, or the training you have gone through, and what you talk about with colleagues, you will be more or less aware of motivation theories.

Just to emphasise the validity of the seven skills described here will you list those theories below (you may be pleasantly surprised at how much you know). Then ask yourself this:

> Which of those theories does not support, or even goes against, the seven skills in the framework of Practical Leadership Skills?

The Theories	Which of the seven skills are not supported?

Skill No. 7, "Always set a specific follow-up date", is seldom covered quite so specifically, but well-balanced theories will cover all the others in one way or another.

WHERE ARE WE NOW?

---

1. MAINTAIN OR ENHANCE THE SELF-ESTEEM OF THE EMPLOYEE.

---

2. Don't attack the person, FOCUS ON THE PROBLEM.

3. Don't assume that the employee has committed an offence.

4. Encourage the employee to express their opinions and make suggestions.

5. Allow the employee adequate time to think through the problem and to suggest a solution.

6. Ensure that the employee has an appropriate ACTION programme.

7. Always set a specific follow-up date.

SKILL 1.

MAINTAIN OR ENHANCE THE SELF-ESTEEM OF THE EMPLOYEE.

Many things affect the way employees feel about themselves and different influences come into play at different times. But most employees have one constant in their lives: their manager. And, as Peter Drucker has said,[1]

> "A manager develops people. Through the way he manages he makes it easy or difficult for them to develop themselves. He directs people or mis-directs them. He brings out what is in them or he stifles them. He strengthens their integrity or he corrupts them. He trains them to stand upright or he deforms them."

How do you feel about that statement? Where would you put yourself on this scale? Just write in an X.

Strongly
agree?

Strongly
disagree?

You will come back to this later.

"But anyway," you might say, "are people not responsible for their own lives?" Of course they are, but there is no getting away from the fact that YOU influence the way they feel about themselves and, therefore, the way they go about their work and their working relationships.

People with good self-esteem are confident "can-do" people, they get on with things; those with low self-esteem tend to find problems rather than solutions. So you *must* be in the business of building people up, enhancing their self-esteem; at the very least you are maintaining it. You are definitely not in the business of putting people down.

---

[1]   From "The Effective Executive" by Peter F. Drucker, Pan Books 1967

There are many ways you can use this skill in face-to-face discussions. And, away from face-to-face situations, "Maintain or enhance the self-esteem of the employee" becomes the management philosophy and practices that you follow. See what you can work out from the options below.

Take two minutes to decide which of the following are valid ways of "maintaining or enhancing the self-esteem of the employee". For each item tick one *or more* of:

'M' for maintains self-esteem,

'E' for enhances self-esteem, or

'N' for neither.

As you do that, consider what your own practice is.

Ways to maintain or enhance self-esteem?	M	E	N
1. Remind people of their successes when they feel bad about mistakes.			
2. Give feedback on *dependable* performance (not just outstanding work). And on poor performance too.			
3. Ensure employees know how they contribute to the team and to the organisation.			
4. Tell people they are doing really well even if they are not.			

Comments are on the next page.

Comments

	'M' for maintains self-esteem, 'E' for enhances, or 'N' for neither.	M	E	N
1.	Remind people of their successes when they feel bad about a mistake.	✓	✓	
	We all make mistakes, and when people feel a bit down it's nice to have a little lift. And this is good for you too. Plus, if they are not feeling too low, you may wish to see what they have learned from the mistake.			
2.	Give feedback on *dependable* performance (not just outstanding work). And on poor performance too.	✓	✓	
	Giving positive feedback keeps good performance coming. People know what you expect in this area and may even try to improve. Feedback on poor performance, again showing your standards, will generally bring improvement, with less worry for the employee and thus better self-esteem.			
3.	Ensure employees know how they contribute to the team and to the organisation.		✓	
	Good teamwork brings job satisfaction. Plus, people supporting their colleagues can expect support in return.			
4.	Tell people they are doing really well even if they are not.		✓	✓
	If they have done really well to get to where they are, a pat on the back is encouraging. BUT, if your remarks indicated they were already up to standard, a later attempt to raise performance may lead to recriminations.			

Why not write your own comments in this panel?

There are more questions overleaf.

We're still on questions about self-esteem of your people.

Take two more minutes to decide which of the following are valid ways of "maintaining or enhancing the self-esteem of the employee". For each item tick one *or more* of:

 'M' for maintains,   'E' for enhances, or   'N' for neither.

As you do that, consider what your own practice is.

Ways to maintain or enhance self-esteem?	M	E	N
5. When people get something wrong tell them, "Never mind, you did your best."			
6. Maintain an open and consistent management style (by, for example, applying these Practical Leadership Skills).			
7. Share with employees any credit which comes to you as the team leader.			
8. Set high standards; train and equip employees accordingly.			

Comments on the questions are over the page.

Here's a thought for you:

"Man's mind, stretched to a new idea, never goes back to its original dimensions"

Oliver Wendell Holmes

Comments

	'M' for maintains self-esteem, 'E' for enhances, or 'N' for neither.	M	E	N
5.	When people get something wrong tell them, "Never mind, you did your best."	✓		✓
	You don't want people feeling bad for trying something new. But nor do you want them to feel that activity matters more than achievement. Help them to learn from the problem - and feel better.			
6.	Maintain an open and consistent management style (by, for example, applying these Practical Leadership Skills).	✓	✓	
	When people know what to expect from you, they'll feel more able to approach you and they'll probably know the limits of what they can do.			
7.	Share with employees any credit which comes to you as the team leader.		✓	
	You're only as good as your team. And if a team leader does not acknowledge the contributions that people make what is likely to happen?			
8.	Set high standards; train and equip employees accordingly.		✓	
	When people take pride in a job well done it's their way of taking pride in themselves. Even the most mundane jobs and tasks may have adverse consequences if they are not done well.			

Before you move to the questions on the next page, how are you doing so far? A note in the margin?

More questions to help you think about people and your own management practices.

Take two more minutes to decide which of the following are valid ways of "maintaining or enhancing the self-esteem of the employee". For each item tick one *or more* of:

'M' for maintains,   'E' for enhances, or   'N' for neither.

Ways to maintain or enhance self-esteem?	M	E	N
9. Aim for satisfaction through achievement, rather than for happiness and contentment.			
10. Help your people to share a vision of what can be achieved.			
11. Ensure conditions are right for the performance that you demand of people.			
12. Help your people to keep up to date so that they will be able to handle the future.			

Comments are on the next page.

Here's another thought for you.

"You cannot teach a man anything. You can only help him discover it for himself."

Galileo

Comments

	'M' for maintains self-esteem, 'E' for enhances, or 'N' for neither.	M	E	N
9.	Aim for satisfaction through achievement, rather than for happiness and contentment.	✓	✓	

Achievement provides the livelihood. Coasting along leaves people - and the organisation - vulnerable to change and competition.

		M	E	N
10.	Help your people to share a vision of what can be achieved.	✓	✓	

It doesn't have to be complicated. It can be as simple as, "We want to be the best at what we do."

Or, "We want to make customers not just happy, but delighted."

		M	E	N
11.	Ensure conditions are right for the performance that you demand of people.	✓	✓	

If they have to work with inadequate equipment or poor quality materials they may not be able to do the good job that they can take pride in. On the other hand, triumphing in adverse conditions can also be a source of pride - but for how long?

		M	E	N
12.	Help your people to keep up to date so that they will be able to handle the future.	✓	✓	

And they can contribute more to current work as well. With the pace of change people can worry about falling behind. Good training and development have always been valuable aids to recruiting good people.

More than a few ticks now.

13.   "Be understanding of failure."

In the context of, "Maintain or enhance the self-esteem of the employee", what do you think of that statement - and why?

Will you write your answer in the box below?

---

14.   "But, for goodness' sake," some managers may say, "these things are not important for my staff. What matters most to them is pay, first and last."

Now, you may not say that but what do you think of the statement, and why?

Will you write your answer in the box below?

Comments are on the next page.

Comments

13. "Be understanding of failure." In the context of, "Maintain or enhance the self-esteem of the employee", what do you think of that statement - and why?

Nothing ventured, nothing gained. No failures means no attempts at new things. There are some tips later for reducing the chance of failure, or at least the scale of it.

So the occasional failure should be seen in the context of other successes, and also as a learning process (but let us learn from our successes too).

Understanding reasons for failure is *not* the same as condoning failure; that's not on. Failing to learn from mistakes should also be a rare occurrence and should earn less understanding.

14. "But, for goodness' sake," some managers may say, "these things are not important for my staff. What matters most to them is pay, first and last."

Now, you may not say that but what do you think of the statement, and why?

People come to work for the money that the job provides, of course they do. But once they walk through the door in the morning (or at the start of the week or month) their pay is pretty well assured. So once they are *at* work their potential is there for the boss to use or to suppress.

This is not to say that money is not important. If, for example, one employee perceives that another is better paid for the same or lesser work, then the money issue becomes a *de*motivator. We'll take another look at this sort of thing shortly.

Ask yourself this

Consider how each of these questions applies to you.

15. Individuals. Do you have any staff who work in isolation, or who may be subject to bullying, teasing or harassment? What is the effect on them?

    Run through a mental checklist of your people.

    Do you need to take action? What should it be?

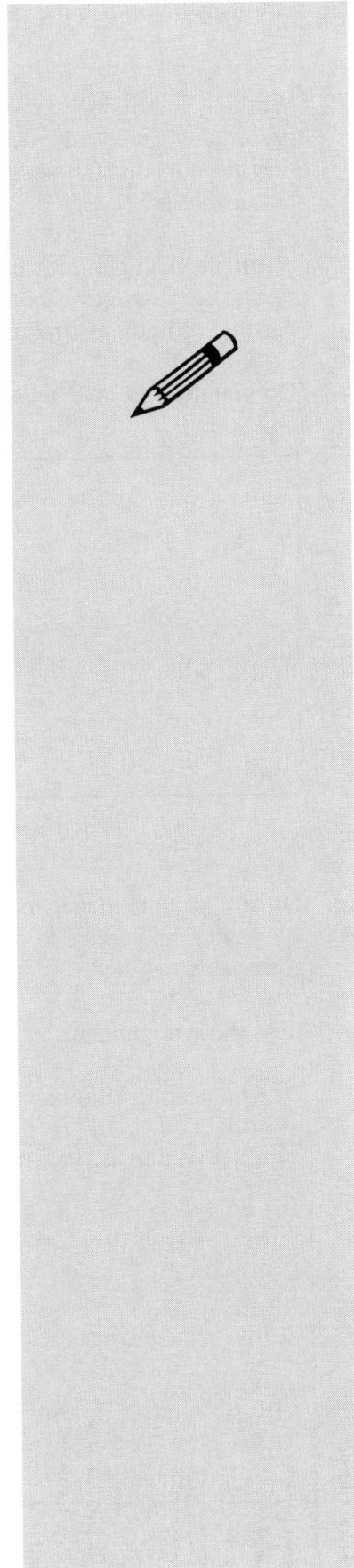

16. The resources that influence the productivity of your people: are any not up to the job? For example, some new software runs very slowly on quite recent computers which are otherwise in perfect order.

    If people are expected to work with indequate resources what may they think about your view of them, or the importance of their work?

    Do you need to take action? What should it be?

No comments but two more questions.

17. Working conditions. Are there any conditions, rules or procedures which may deter people from doing what they need to do? Or which get in the way of doing a reasonable job?

    A simple example: lack of organised storage space so that work spaces become cluttered and things become difficult to find, or easy to overlook.

    Do you need to take action? What should it be?

18. Do any (senior) managers talk one way but act another, eg, paying lip service to quality, value for money, customer care, etc?

    If so, how might staff be affected?

    Do you need to take action? What should it be?

Some specific practices

Providing feedback and recognition does *not* mean that you have to go around giving feedback and recognition all the time. Nor does it mean that these things wait for the Annual Performance Review.

Naturally, it helps if your staff - and you - are agreed on what they are supposed to do, so the next three questions focus on specific practices that give people a measure of freedom whilst not reducing necessary control.

---

19. To what extent do your people have *agreed standards of performance* in the key areas of their jobs? Focus on KEY areas of the job, not minute-to-minute detail. (Standards of performance = output measured, depending on the work, over periods of an hour, day, week, month or year.)

    0%   100%

---

20. To what extent do they have *objectives* relating to continuous job improvement?
    (Objective = a task, goal or target with a cut-off date.)

    0%   100%

---

21. To what extent do they get feedback on how well they are doing against both types of goal? (Do they have regular information enabling them to assess and adjust their performance *without* your intervention?)

    0%   100%

Still on specific practices.

---

22. To what extent do your people have the training and development needed to perform to the levels required now - and to those that will apply in the future?

0%   100%

---

23. Consider how you, or someone you know, may have been affected by some bosses in the past, eg, how did you work, and how did you feel, with a poor boss who was always critical and never gave recognition for a job well done?

    And how did you feel - and work - when you gained a sense of achievement through the way another boss managed you?

        Was there a difference?   YES   NO

        Was it important to you?   YES   NO

    Circle the one that applies.

A quick review now.

Will you please turn back to page 12 where you were asked to indicate what you thought of the statement by Peter Drucker in his book, "The Effective Executive".

If you were on the left of the scale you probably feel that this section of the book endorses your view; quite right too. If you were to the right do you want to move left?

Questions you have been wanting to ask

24. "What if someone needs taking down a peg or two?"

    This is a common question in workshops on these skills. So, in the context of, "Maintain or enhance the self-esteem of the employee", what do you think?

    ```

    ```

25. "What about when you have to give someone a telling-off, or when you have to discipline them?"

    In fact, those are two separate questions and both are valid. So how would you answer them with, "Maintain or enhance the self-esteem of the employee" in mind?

    a. "What about when you have to give someone a telling-off?"

    b. "What about when you have to discipline them?"

Comments are on the next page.

Comments

24. "What if someone needs taking down a peg or two?"

Check out the next skill, "Don't attack the person, focus on the problem."

More answers lie in another book in this series on dealing with unacceptable performance, something which can cause much stress - for both boss and employee.

But if the question arises because an employee seems over confident, even frighteningly so, what is wrong with that? Why not turn all that self-confidence to good account with a challenging work assignment?

25a. "What about when you have to give someone a telling-off?"

Sorry to sound glib but see the first two paragraphs of the comment above.

b. "Or when you have to discipline them?"

The severity of the discipline is important here. If the discipline is dismissal then the person ceases to be your employee.

Anything short of dismissal means that the employee will be continuing to work for you and you want, at least, to maintain their self-esteem.

There are ways of doing that and, because this is an important area which can have serious ramifications, there is another book in the series which deals with just this problem.

Practice makes perfect

You can practise this skill in ways which compliment each other.

   a.   Through what you say (or don't say) to people; some of the earlier questions and comments indicate fruitful areas.

   b.   Through the way you manage, your practices, what you do, how you arrange things.

26. Would you take another couple of minutes to scan the earlier pages and circle below the numbers of those questions where your responses prompt you to action.

1	2	3	4
5	6	7	8
9	10	11	12
13	14	15	16
17	18	19	20
21	22	23	24
25a	25b		

27. And what other ways can you think of to "Maintain or enhance the self-esteem of the employee"?

Finally

A.   Do you ever ask for, and receive, extra time from some of your people without giving recognition in some form or other?

```



```

B.   Of all the things within this skill that you intend to do, which single one will have the most impact?

```



```

C.   Having looked at what this skill covers, are there any *individuals* to whom you now want to pay particular attention?

```



```

As you work through Skills 2 to 7 you'll see how they all contribute towards Number One, "Maintain or enhance the self-esteem of the employee".

To summarise: You're in the business of building people up, not knocking them down.

WHERE ARE WE NOW?

1.   Maintain or enhance the self-esteem of the employee.   √

---

2.   DON'T ATTACK THE PERSON,

FOCUS ON THE PROBLEM.

---

3.   Don't assume that the employee has committed an offence.

4.   Encourage the employee to express their opinions and make
        suggestions.

5.   Allow the employee adequate time to think through the problem
        and to suggest a solution.

6.   Ensure that the employee has an appropriate action programme.

7.   Always set a specific follow-up date.

SKILL 2.

DON'T ATTACK THE PERSON, FOCUS ON THE PROBLEM.

When things go wrong it is easy to attack the person responsible. But if *you* feel attacked, how do you react?

You will have seen how some people get their hackles up and attack back; the problem then takes a back seat, tempers flare, things are said and later regretted. And you will have seen how, at the end of a stressful quarrel, the problem is still not resolved.

You'll also have seen how other people back off; they appear to give in but then, having suffered in silence during an attack, they want to "get their own back" to rebuild their self-esteem. Their later behaviour may be passive but very satisfying; like letting the boss or other members of the team walk into problems, or failing to offer constructive ideas when they are badly needed.

Attacking people, that is with intent to hurt, defeat, demoralise, is counter-productive. It also takes valuable time and energy - which good bosses value. They believe most people come to work to do a good job and know that if an employee does something which is really unacceptable they can handle that.

Focusing on the problem is much more productive but, nevertheless, can be hard to do. So remember, the problem you define is the problem you solve. Define the problem wrongly and you will get the wrong solution. Then, after a lot of work, the original problem is still there. Solutions to problems are like keys in locks, if they don't fit they don't work!

Focusing on the problem also helps to avoid attacking the person. And when people feel uncomfortable for making mistakes they will be grateful to you for this.

Focusing on the problem helps to keep people on track too; when you're in a meeting and people get off the point it can be very useful to ask, "How does that help with solving the problem?"

Focusing on the problem gets results! And many problems are positive ones, for example, how to take advantage of an opportunity, or set new targets. ("The problem is, how to become the best in our field?") Other problems present opportunities for change!

All of the following are ways to avoid attacking the person and/or focus on the problem. Which is which? Tick in one or both columns.

Ways to avoid attacking the person and/or focus on the problem.	Avoids attacking the person	Focuses on the problem
1. Trying to see mistakes from the perspective of what needs to be done for correction, rather than laying blame for the error.		
2. Encouraging people to be open with each other but to choose their words carefully - so they are factual, precise and objective.		
3. Understanding the dividing line between being vigorous and being nasty.		
4. Remembering that tackling the wrong problem means finishing with the wrong solution.		

Comments are on the next page.

Comments

Ways to avoid attacking the person and/or focus on the problem.	Avoids attacking the person	Focuses on the problem
1. Seeking to correct mistakes rather than allocating blame.	✓	✓
You focus, not on the person as a problem, but on fixing the WORK problem in their area of responsibility. Attacking an employee would be an abusive indulgence; you would not attack a non-employee.		
2. Encouraging openness coupled with objectivity.	✓	✓
And knowing that when there is a problem most people want to understand the cause (or the background to the opportunity) and find a solution.		
3. Understanding the dividing line between being vigorous and being nasty.	✓	✓
Vigour helps to solve problems; nastiness hurts people. Negative feedback, *given objectively*, is not a personal attack, even if forceful, but a starting point for corrective action.		
4. Remembering that tackling the wrong problem means finishing with the wrong solution.		✓
Helping to clarify a problem could be the major role of the boss, the solution may then be obvious to the employee. Remember, solutions to problems are like keys in locks; if they don't fit they don't work. So be specific and ask others to be specific too.		

We are still looking at ways to avoid attacking the person and/or to focus on the problem. There are more questions to help examine this important skill.

Will you take a couple of minutes to look at these four?

Ways to avoid attacking the person and/or focus on the problem.	Avoids attacking the person	Focuses on the problem
5. Knowing that people are often better at some types of work than others. Being good at some things means that they may be less good at others.		
6. Thinking of "focus" as you would with a camera, that is, making things sharp and clear (fuzzy problems get fuzzy solutions).		
7. Listening well so that, by asking appropriate questions, and prompting, you can help people to clarify problems.		
8. Sorting out a "can of worms" into its separate parts. Then handling these smaller problems one at a time.		

Comments are on the next page.

Comments

Ways to avoid attacking the person and/or focus on the problem.	Avoids attacking the person	Focuses on the problem
5. Knowing that people are often better at some types of work than others. Being good at some things means that they may be less good at others.	✓	
Accepting that few people can do everything well means you can be more forgiving of mistakes. You may also try to arrange for people to do more of what they are good at and less of the other stuff.		
6. Thinking of "focus" as with a camera, that is, making things sharp and clear (fuzzy problems get fuzzy solutions).		✓
Then you can pick out what is important in the picture and concentrate on that.		
7. Listening well so that, by asking appropriate questions, or prompting, you can help people to clarify problems.	✓	✓
After your questions the word "summarise" could be useful here. For example, "So what you're saying is that you need a way to . . . "		
8. Sorting out a "can of worms" into its separate parts. Then these smaller problems can be handled one at a time.		✓
And solving just one of the small separated problems may help with several of the others.		

Four more questions on ways to avoid attacking the person and/or to focus on the problem.

Ways to avoid attacking the person and/or focus on the problem.	Avoids attacking the person	Focuses on the problem
9. Knowing that people with agreed goals (standards, targets) have a better context for approaching and solving problems.		
10. Confronting barriers to good teamwork, for example, when the team is not facing up to an issue, or are not being objective and specific.		
11. Ensuring, when making a decision, that you look at *what* is right not *who* is right.		
12. Recognising that people may argue strongly for their preferred solution to a problem, and they should not be attacked for this.		

Comments are on the next page but meantime:

> *"There is no way"*
>   *denies the possibility of invention.*

Comments

Ways to avoid attacking the person and/or focus on the problem.	Avoids attacking the person	Focuses on the problem
9. Knowing that people with agreed goals have a better context for approaching and solving problems.		✓
They are more likely to ask, "What are we trying to achieve?" as a way of moving to problem solutions.		
10. Confronting barriers to good teamwork, for example, when the team is not facing up to an issue, or are being vague.	✓	✓
If team members are avoiding an issue or talking in woolly terms they need to be brought back to the "objective" mode. Bringing things into the open is less uncomfortable in the long run than living with concealed tensions.		
11. Ensuring, when making a decision, that you look at *what* is right not *who* is right.		✓
If you agree *criteria* for what a good choice will give you, it is easier to choose between competing options. See the next question and comments.		
12. Accepting that people argue for their own solution to a problem, and should not be attacked for this.	✓	
This highlights the need for an open decison-making process. Then, if anyone becomes too attached to their own proposal they can be asked to check it against the criteria for a successful decision.		

Some problems, caused by managers but blamed on employees, can lead to attacks due to exasperation.

13. Have you ever known an employee's initial training to be curtailed because of pressure of work, covering for someone's absence, that sort of thing? In your experience what sort of problems can that cause?

14. Have you ever known an employee to be trained up on a range of tasks but then not perform some of them? Then, after a while, a manager wants the employee to do something which is now long forgotten? But the manager firmly believes the employee *can* do what they are being asked to do. What is likely to happen?

15. Have you ever known mistakes occur because of shortage of time, bad planning, lack of information for the employee, or lack of consultation with them? Many such mistakes can be avoided by better management of time. The paradox is that managers who cannot find time to get things right in the first place do have time (usually at the expense of some other job) to put things right later. What examples can you note?

All the above problems lend themselves to simple and fairly obvious solutions (at least, they seem obvious after we got things wrong the first time). Better thinking prevents them.

Here you can use another common problem cause to look at possible problem areas in your own work situation.

Some problems of omission or commission occur because, for the employee involved, doing the right thing doesn't seem to be important. It may be important to *you*, but it isn't important to *them*.

This can be really vexing for the boss but, if people don't get positive feedback when they do a good job, or negative feedback when they err, why should they bother? If something doesn't seem to matter to you why should it matter to them?

16. Briefly put yourself in the shoes of each of your people and ask yourself which of them would be likely to give you improved performance in response to negative or positive feedback from you.

    Note their initials and performance areas below.

Making good performance matter, one way or the other, is one of the fundamental skills for managers. Appropriate feedback, in good time, helps to prevent small problems becoming larger ones. Whichever method you need to use, you are showing why something is important. Sometimes employees may not know that.

A good way to focus people on the problem is to ask them to *describe what they are getting* that they don't like. Ask questions of the What? Who? Where? When? How? and Why? variety.

That takes them from the perhaps vague to the quite precise. The next step is to ask them to *specify what they want*, again in precise terms, and being realistic rather than idealistic.

Then ask why the difference (between what they're getting and what they want) is important. Note the open question: *"Why* is it important?", not *"Is* it important?", because that just gets a quick "Yes".

At this point unimportant problems can be set aside (they may be *annoying* but you really need to deal with things that are important).

17. Now; do you need to coach any of your people to be more focused when raising problems? If so, who and why? Note their names and other information. (What about yourself?)

We have briefly looked at one way, summarised here, of setting aside unimportant concerns and focusing on things that matter:

Describing the Difference

Describe	Specify
what you're getting.	what you want.
↓	↓

Ask *why* the difference is important.

"Describing the Difference" can be useful in looking at anything where you think you want to change performance. Doing it can help in avoiding what is described below.

In your experience have you ever known problems to be tackled in haste?

Of course you have, that's the nature of some problem circumstances, so let's focus a little more tightly.

18. Have you ever known a situation where the first idea for solving a problem was implemented without further thought? And then went wrong? Please write in here a short description of the situation.

```



```

Was the solution wrong because (a) the problem *cause was not properly established*? Or was it wrong because (b) it just didn't suit the problem?

```



```

It's a rare manager who can't write something in these two boxes; some personal life decisions come in this category.

Previous questions highlight what you know already; that some problems are not caused by employees, so attacking them, instead of focusing on the problem, is simply not fair.

Ask yourself this

19. If a boss is observed to attack an employee, how might that affect the authority or acceptance of the boss?

20. If an employee feels, rightly or wrongly, that they have been attacked, they may try to get back at the boss, or the team, or the organisation in order to restore their self-esteem.

    In your own work situation what ways are there for people to "get their own back"? Think of active ways and of passive ways.

So, besides being unfair, attacking an employee can have adverse consequences.

Questions you have been wanting to ask

Take your time with these two questions before you read the comments below.

21. One question that comes up quite often in workshops is, "Does this mean that I can't ever lose my temper?" In the context of "Don't attack the person, **focus on the problem**", how would you answer that question?

22. And another question is, "Sometimes you need to be forceful in order to really jolt the person. Could that be seen as an attack?"

Comments

21. The most frequent response to this question is, "If you lose your temper, you lose control."

22. Forcefulness is fine as long as it doesn't turn into an attack. *Controlled* anger is akin to forcefulness, jolting someone in order to provoke determination and action - given in Skill No. 6, " · · · action programme."

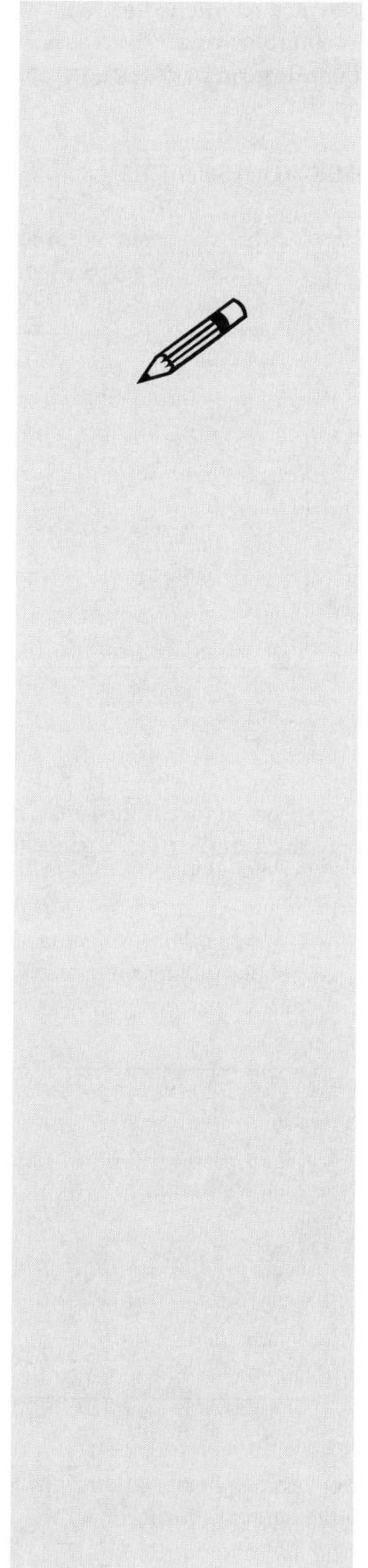

Practice makes perfect

This is an important skill requiring self-awareness and self-control on the one hand, with good coaching skills and determination on the other. You can practise this skill in ways which compliment each other.

23. Please take a couple of minutes to scan the earlier pages in this section and circle below the numbers of those questions where your responses will serve as reminders and/or prompt you to action.

1	2	3	4
5	6	7	8
9	10	11	12
13	14	15	16
17	18	19	20
	21	22	

24. Does,

"Don't attack the person,
focus on the problem"

prompt any other thoughts or intentions at the moment?

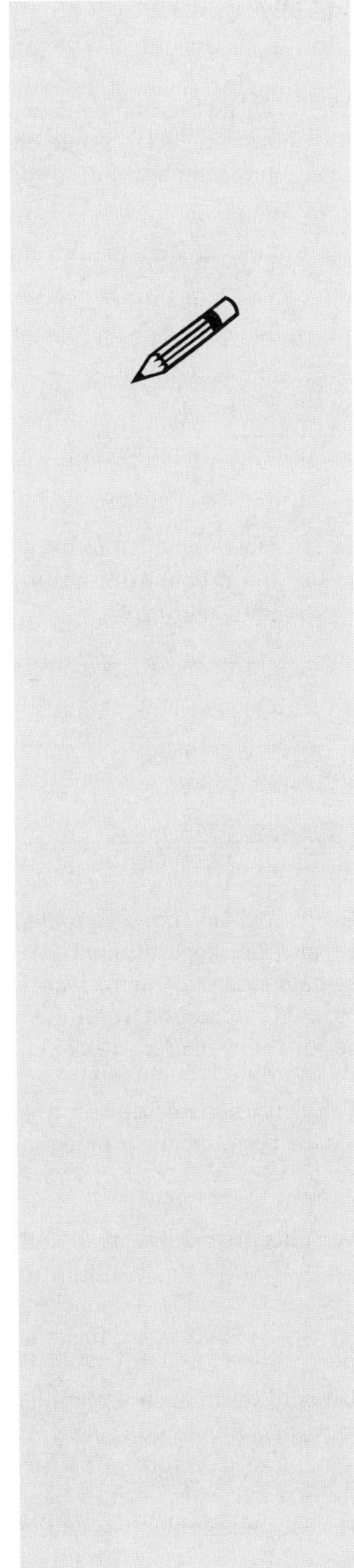

Finally

25.   Of all the problems you may have looked at in this
        section which single one, if solved, will have the
        most impact?

```
┌─────────────────────────────────────────┐
│                                           │
│                                           │
│                                           │
│                                           │
│                                           │
└─────────────────────────────────────────┘
```

26.   Having looked at what this skill covers, are there any
        individuals with whom you now want to take
        particular care?

```
┌─────────────────────────────────────────┐
│                                           │
│                                           │
│                                           │
└─────────────────────────────────────────┘
```

Deeper examination of problem analysis techniques is
beyond the scope of this book, but probably the most
common cause of performance problems with people is
covered in question 16 in this section, about making good
performance matter - to the employee as well as to you.

The other skills described in this book can also help to
reduce performance problems.

To summarise this section, both parts of

> "Don't attack the person,
> **focus on the problem**"

can help enormously in building effective working relationships. So, if ever you find yourself getting wound up, and
wanting to give someone a piece of your mind, remember
the first part. Also that, if people feel they are not liable to
be attacked, problems get solved, not covered up.

WHERE ARE WE NOW?

1. Maintain or enhance the self-esteem of the employee.   √

2. Don't attack the person, FOCUS ON THE PROBLEM.   √

---

3.   DON'T ASSUME THAT THE EMPLOYEE HAS COMMITTED AN OFFENCE.

---

4. Encourage the employee to express their opinions and make suggestions.

5. Allow the employee adequate time to think through the problem and to suggest a solution.

6. Ensure that the employee has an appropriate action programme.

7. Always set a specific follow-up date.

SKILL 3.

DON'T ASSUME THAT THE EMPLOYEE HAS COMMITTED AN OFFENCE.

You need to be aware of this skill in two ways.

First is when people become angry when something goes wrong. You hear someone say, "He's really let me down" or, "Just wait 'til I get hold of him". Then, with mind made up, they don't seek an explanation. Or, if the employee tries to explain, they listen, but not well - or not at all.

It may be *prudent* to *suspect* someone has made a *mistake*, but if you turn suspicions into assumptions you get tunnel vision and see nothing beyond your assumptions about the cause of the problem.

An "offence" is something done in a *wilful, malicious, or neglectful* manner, and this must be rare. So if you find yourself being very angry or contemptuous of someone ("What can you expect?") you may be assuming the worst.

Second is when you feel apprehensive or pessimistic about dealing with someone. We can get wrong ideas about some people or groups of people and we can also bring some unconscious assumptions to work with us. For example, if we assume that people prefer a comfortable life we may hesitate to require a higher standard of performance or a greater contribution of ideas. If we assume that people cannot help with a problem we don't ask for help.

Sometimes, if someone questions our thinking we may assume disloyalty, whereas the employee may just not understand, or has sensible reservations. Because such a person doesn't "go along" like everyone else we may assume they "don't fit in". In fact, that person may be the team's only source of new ideas.

If we can make such wrongful assumptions what does that say about our regular view of the people involved? Are we constantly fearful of being let down? Are we afraid of delegating because staff can't be trusted? Is this really due to their ineptitude or to our own assumptions that they are less than competent?

And then there are unconscious assumptions; more later.

A quick question now to establish just how important assumptions can be. You'll need just a minute or so.

Imagine a colleague saying something which indicated a wrong assumption about you.

1. a. How would you react? And

    b. How would it affect your view of that person and the way you work with them?

a.

b.

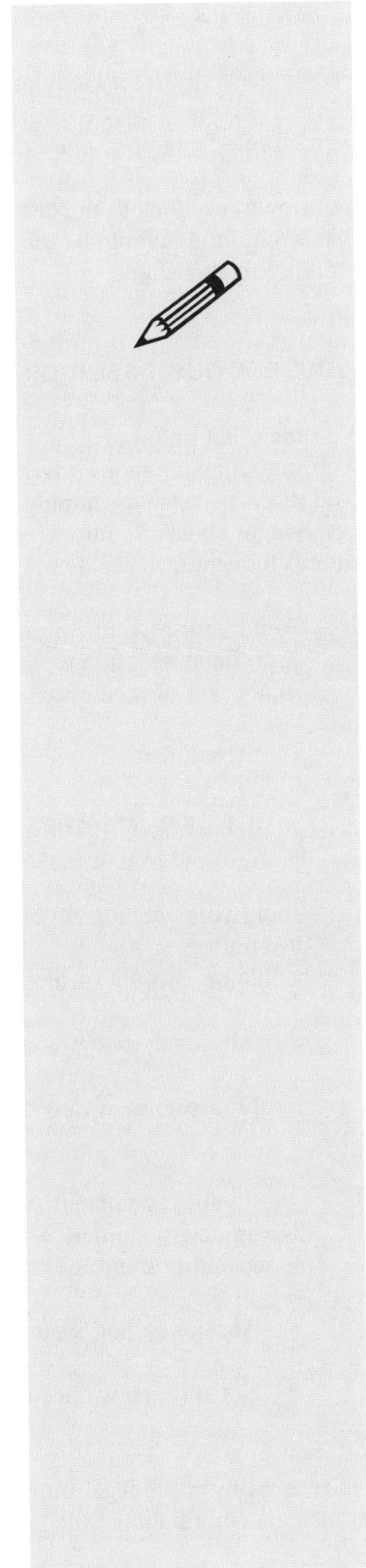

See the next page for comments.

Comments

People generally react badly to wrongful assumptions about themselves; these can be revealed in chance remarks, badly worded questions or in one's actions.

Your own reactions to the last question will have indicated that wrongful assumptions can seriously damage one's working relationships.

Unconscious assumptions

You may, but only may, have written or unwritten policies with inbuilt assumptions which have been around for years. And, because these assumptions are unconscious, they never get thought about. So now is a good a time to give some careful thought to these questions.

2. Could your recruitment and/or promotion policies be discriminating - in any way at all - against good people on account of their race? Please circle one.

    Absolutely not, we check all the time.

    Not sure, so we need to check carefully.

3. Could your recruitment and/or promotion policies be discriminating - in any way at all - against good people on account of their sex? Please circle one.

    Absolutely not, we check all the time.

    Not sure, so we need to check carefully.

4. Could your recruitment and/or promotion policies be discriminating - in any way at all - against good people on account of their age or disability? Please circle one.

    Absolutely not, we check all the time.

    Not sure, so we need to check carefully.

Quite apart from the legal implications it would be a shame to lose the contribution which good people can make.

Another trouble with assumptions is that they can turn out to be self-fulfilling prophecies, for example, you assume someone will be awkward with you so you treat them in a less friendly manner. They then respond badly and you can see they are awkward - as you predicted!

Or you assume that employees are not interested in the organisation's problems or its direction, so you keep them in the dark. And, sure enough, they become uninterested and they lack initiative.

Which of the following would HELP you to avoid making wrong assumptions? Please tick as appropriate.

Would help or not help to avoid making wrong assumptions?	Helps	Does not help
5. *Knowing*, when something goes wrong, that it may be prudent to *suspect* a mistake but you must still check it out.		
6. *Being open* with people about what might be worrying you and prepared to confront problems in an objective manner.		
7. *Realising* that anger is often brought on by quick, and wrong, assumptions.		
8. *Knowing* that people are not trying to be obstructive when they question ideas; that they contribute to good teamwork in their different ways.		

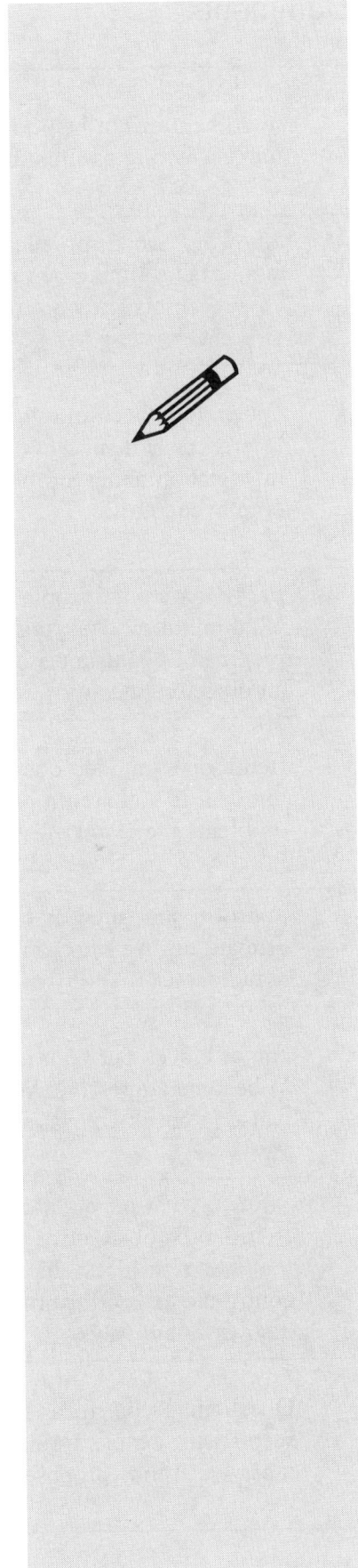

Comments are on the next page.

Comments

Would help or not help to avoid making wrong assumptions?	Helps	Does not help
5. *Knowing*, when something goes wrong, that it may be prudent to *suspect* a mistake but you must still check it out.	✓	
When you check out your suspicions, avoid inferences and stick to observable facts; seek the information about a problem which only the employee knows.		
6. *Being open* with people about what might be worrying you and prepared to confront problems in an objective manner.	✓	
Being open-minded does not mean being empty-minded. If you are prepared to objectively confront problems they won't fester and create more tension.		
7. *Realising* that anger is often brought on by quick, and wrong, assumptions.	✓	
Anger blocks out your ability to listen, or causes you to become aggressive. When you feel that way, pause to check your assumptions.		
8. *Knowing* that people are not trying to be obstructive when they question ideas; that they contribute to good teamwork in their different ways.	✓	
Questioning your ideas shows interest or (healthy) scepticism. People are not necessarily ignoring your ideas when they propose their own.		

Four more questions in similar vein.

Would help or not help to avoid making wrong assumptions?	Helps	Does not help
9. *Accepting* that someone who question your decisions, or gives you unwelcome feedback, is not necessarily out to undermine you.		
10. *Appreciating* that some people may not be skilled teamworkers, for example, they don't acknowledge what's good with an idea before raising problems with it - to the proposer's dismay.		
11. *Being prepared*, as a general rule, to find that people are stupid - but being on the lookout for exceptions to the rule.		
12. *Reviewing* with yourself the reasons why you dislike or feel unable to trust someone.		

Comments are on the next page.

> This seems a good place for another thought:
>
> *"When you think you are arguing with an idiot, so does he."*

Comments

Would help or not help to avoid making wrong assumptions?	Helps	Does not help
9. *Accepting* that someone who questions your decisions, or gives you unwelcome feedback, is not necessarily out to undermine you.	✓	
But they should be specific in their questioning and objective in their feedback.		
10. *Appreciating* that some people may not be skilled team-workers, for example, they don't acknowledge what's good with an idea before raising problems with it - to the proposer's dismay.	✓	
And it is for you to help them raise the level of their teamwork skills, either through formal training or through personal coaching.		
11. *Being prepared*, as a general rule, to find that people are stupid - but being on the lookout for exceptions to the rule.		✓
This was included only to highlight again the earlier piece about self-fulfilling prophecies (top of p 49).		
12. *Reviewing* with yourself the reasons why you dislike or feel unable to trust someone.	✓	
We can all take a dislike to someone for some reason and eventually forget why. But the dislike lingers on. If we can't remember the reason it can't have been important. Let's start again.		

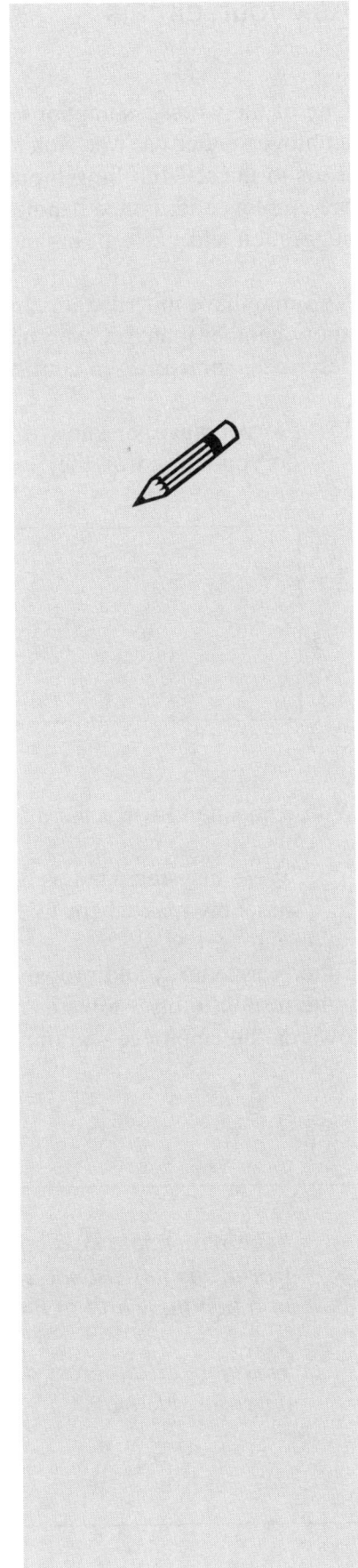

Looking at your own work situation now.

13. a.   Would you say that you have less regard for some of your employees than others?

b.   If so, is that lower regard based on recent *objective* evidence or on old prejudice, hearsay or rumour, innuendo or gossip?

c.   Whatever the reason, do you ever let this lower regard affect you in any way?

d.   What steps should you take, if any, to correct any wrongful assumptions?

a.

b.

c.

d.

14. a.   Do members of your team sometimes express reservations (or stronger) about members of any other team?

b.   If so, and because that might interfere with effective working relationships, what should be done about tackling each situation of this kind?

a.

b.

Ask yourself this

One of the worst assumptions a manager can make is that an employee either can't or won't contribute ideas. Again this leads to the self-fulfilling prophecy. The cause may be that the employee was once handled badly when making a suggestion and has kept his mouth shut ever since.

You may have inherited an employee like this, or you may know another manager who has one, an employee who is described, sometimes in confidence, as dead wood.

15. Do you have, or know of, anyone like that? If you do, do you know *why* they are as they are?

With someone like that the question is,

"Were they recruited as dead wood, or did we somehow make them like that?"

Either way, you would probably agree that the manager has some responsibility - towards himself, his organisation and towards the employee - to improve matters.

> *"The reasonable man adapts himself to the world; the unreasonable man persists in trying to adapt the world to himself.*
>
> *Therefore all progress depends on the unreasonable man."*
>
> George Bernard Shaw

Questions you have been wanting to ask

Here are two fairly common questions that bear thinking about. Will you take a couple of minutes over them?

16. "What if I've got an employee absolutely cold for something? Assumptions don't come into it." How would you answer that?

17. "What if I firmly believe, with good foundation, that an employee is a really bad person." How would you answer that?

Comments

16. What you should *not* do is stop listening. If the employee should have a good explanation and you didn't seek it, where does that leave you?

17. So bad? This is a little like the dead wood question on the previous page. If the employee is indeed so bad you may still be together because the badness does *not* affect work performance. Otherwise, see the book on changing unacceptable performance.

Practice makes perfect

18. This skill requires a great deal of self-awareness as the assumptions trap is always waiting for you. Please look back over the questions shown below and circle here those where you want to make a special effort.

2	3	4	5
6	7	8	9
10	11	12	13
14	15	16	17

19. If there are any individuals with whom you need to be extra careful - because it's so easy to let suspicions turn into assumptions - who's the one person with whom you must be most careful?

(A code name will do)

Finally

Assuming that the employee *has* committed an offence can be stressful for all concerned; if you find yourself getting angry - or apprehensive about speaking with someone - check your assumptions.

WHERE ARE WE NOW?

1. Maintain or enhance the self-esteem of the employee. √

2. Don't attack the person, FOCUS ON THE PROBLEM. √

3. Don't assume that the employee has committed an offence. √

---

4. ENCOURAGE THE EMPLOYEE TO EXPRESS THEIR OPINIONS AND MAKE SUGGESTIONS.

---

5. Allow the employee adequate time to think through the problem and to suggest a solution.

6. Ensure that the employee has an appropriate action programme.

7. Always set a specific follow-up date.

SKILL 4.

ENCOURAGE THE EMPLOYEE TO EXPRESS THEIR OPINIONS AND MAKE SUGGESTIONS.

At one level this skill is about listening to people.

"Tell me about it," gets people *expressing opinions* about a situation or proposal, and generally talking more openly.

"What do you think we should do?" seeks *suggestions* and gets people thinking of solutions to problems, thereby moving the team forward.

But it is also about the team leader *sharing* responsibility; about an approach to people that *recognises* the contribution they can make; an approach which deliberately attempts to tap the resource that is your team, whether this is all your team together, or a sub-team, or just you and one other.

On the one hand, therefore, it is about *creating the circumstances* in which people can freely contribute their opinions on their situation, on the organisation and on proposals made to them, ie giving feedback; and making suggestions about what should be done - about problems or opportunities. On the other hand it is listening to what they say and taking account of it. This is summarised in the word 'participation', a word which is frequently misunder-stood.

Participation does not mean permissiveness, ie the mistaken belief that team members should be able to do what they want just because they think it is the best course of action or the best policy, etc. The employee can contribute their opinions and suggestions and often the boss will be able to go along with them.

However, there is no taking away from the team leader their accountability for the team's success; sometimes the boss will make a decision which upsets some team members by going against their views. At times like this managers have to remember that they are there for effectiveness, not for popularity.

So whilst members of the team participate in a decision by contributing their thinking towards it, it is the boss who makes the decision on behalf of the team and the organisation. This emphasises again the need to be able to focus well on the problem - to *clarify* the goals, both short and long term.

Employees who are well trained can make more valuable contributions to their team, and thus be more commited to the decision they have influenced.

Here are a few management practices. Some encourage employees to express *opinions*, some encourage *suggestions*, some do *both* and some do *neither*. Can you say which are which with one tick, two ticks, or no ticks?

Which encourage *opinions*, and which encourage *suggestions*?	Encourage opinions	Encourage suggestions
1. Practise good listening and questioning skills; taking notes, when appropriate, to show that you are taking heed.		
2. Ask questions to bring out an employee's reasoning, experience and training - and their creativity.		
3. Build on the good bits of someone's proposal but avoid niggling about the bad bits.		
4. Ignore reservations that people express if they are only small reservations.		

Comments are overleaf.

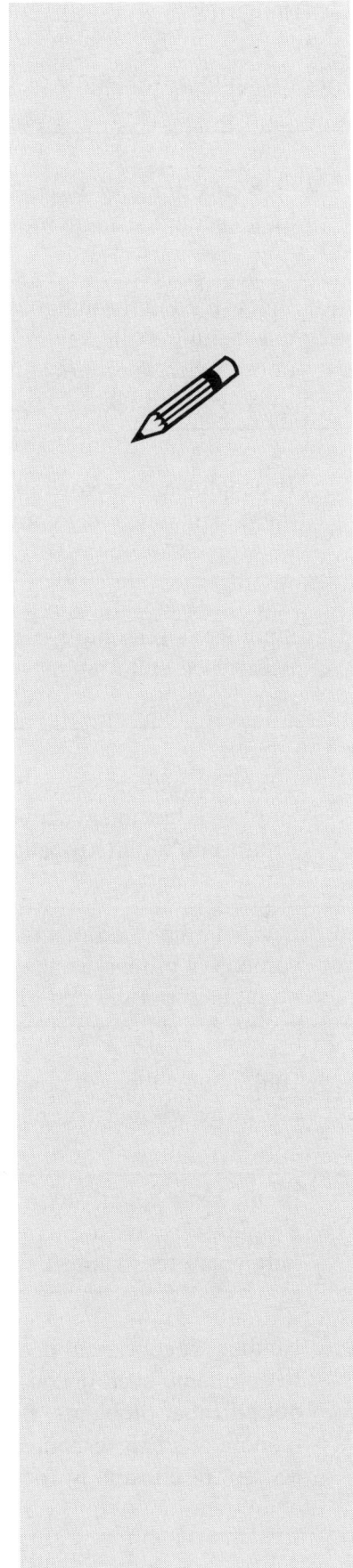

Comments

You may argue with some of these - but that's no bad thing.

Which encourage *opinions,* and which encourage *suggestions?*	Encourage opinions	Encourage suggestions
1. Practise good listening and questioning skills; taking notes, when appropriate, to show you are taking heed.	✓	✓
If people can see you're listening they will talk, so these skills encourage both opinions and suggestions.		
2. Ask questions to bring out an employee's reasoning, experience and training - and their creativity.	✓	✓
Asking questions shows that you value what the employee has to say so you'll get both. But don't let it turn into an interrogation.		
3. Build on the good bits of someone's proposal but avoid niggling about the bad bits.		✓
Building on the good parts means the bad parts can fall away without you having to criticise them.		
4. Ignore reservations that people express if they are only small reservations.		
Neither. Encouraging people to expand on small reservations, even if you don't like them, can bring out potential problems. If they know you are prepared to explore small reservations they are more likely to acccept responsibility for expressing them well.		

These questions are designed to encourage your opinions;
we'll look for your suggestions later.

If you have any ideas as you work through these questions,
write them down in the right-hand panel; don't lose them.

Which encourage *opinions*, and which encourage *suggestions*?	Encourage opinions	Encourage suggestions
5. Be available to answer questions, and to listen to people's ideas, by having an open-door policy.		
6. Ensure your people approach you only with ideas that have been well thought through so that they are presented well.		
7. Train people well - for their own jobs and also so they know the aims of the business and the environment in which it operates.		
8. Share problems with your staff even if you don't understand the cause, or have a solution.		

Comments are overleaf.

Comments

Which encourage *opinions*, and which encourage *suggestions?*	Encourage opinions	Encourage suggestions
5. Being available for questions and ideas through an open-door policy.	✓	✓
An open door policy is fine but walking the job is better. It lets you see what people are talking about, and lets *you* ask questions. It also means that you are not leaving the initiative to others		
6. Ensure your people approach you only with ideas that have been well thought through so that they are presented well.	?	?
Thinking is the hardest work there is. Sometimes half a good idea is better than nothing at all. Ideas that are well presented will obviously save much time for you, but if you have good coaching skills you'll be able to deal with ideas in any form.		
7. Train people well - for their own jobs and also so they know the aims of the business and its environment.	✓	✓
Good training shows the value you place on the people and their work. And they are then better equipped to express opinions and make suggestions.		
8. Share problems with your staff even if you don't understand the cause or have a solution.	✓	✓
You know that you don't have a monopoly on ideas.		

Skills for active listening and questioning

You might almost think that Skill 4, "Encourage the employee to express their opinions and make suggestions", could be summarised in two words, "Listen well".

But it is more than that. "Listening" alone would be too passive but it is still an immensely important skill. Done well, it allows you to employ other skills and, taken together, these all comprise, "Encourage the employee to express their opinions and make suggestions".

Good questions are part of good listening, so let us look now at components of *active* listening and good questioning.

TAKING NOTES

We are not looking for a shorthand record of the conversation, but notes would be useful for . . . what?

9 a.   In what ways can taking notes be useful?

9 b.   In what ways could the taking of notes be counter-productive?

Comments are on the next page.

Comments

9 a.   In what ways can taking notes be useful?

They show you are working at listening, thus showing respect for the employee.

When the speaker realises this he will tend to speak more carefully.

You can note words that you want to come back to, without interrupting the speaker's flow; and without losing the drift yourself.

Writing gives you time to think.

You have a record which you can flesh out later if you wish.

9 b.   In what ways could the taking of notes be counter-productive?

In trying to note too much you could miss something important.

The employee may think you are recording evidence.

So brief notes can be useful, especially in conjunction with some of the other techniques that follow.

FOLLOWING or REFLECTING

Reflecting back the words of the speaker, or the *sense* of their words, *without comment,* is useful with people talking about *their* problems. For example: A person says, "I'm sick and tired of that idiot Fred." You *reflect* what they are saying with, "You're fed up with Fred," or "You think Fred's an idiot."

You make no comment, and you *follow* the speaker, without *leading* the discussion in any particular direction - which could happen if you were to ask questions.

By reflecting, you show you are listening and you encourage more talking. Often, "talking out" a problem is all someone needs to do.

Other ways of following are: nods, eye contact, "I see", "Hm hm", "Go on", etc. And SILENCE. These encourage people to talk, taking pressure off you, and letting you absorb what is important in the information you are receiving.

SUMMARISING

This focuses on the idea or problem as you understand it; and it helps to agree an understanding from which to move forward together, eg, "So what you're saying, I think, is . . ." If you get it wrong the speaker, seeing that you are trying, and *wanting* to be understood, will put you right.

You may or may not need notes to help you with summarising.

EMPATHISING

This shows you understand the person's feelings and helps to get them on your side, eg, "You must be upset." Empathising does NOT necessarily mean that you agree with, or condone, what the speaker is saying. In fact, you may strongly disagree with their views, but it is good to understand how they feel about them.

Empathising is something we tend to do fairly easily, almost unconsciously, in our social lives. At work, however, you may need to work at it.

Taking notes, following/reflecting, summarising and empathising are all part of *active* listening but, to get the full story, the opinions or suggestions, you will also need to be good with questions.

QUESTIONS

These must be used correctly or they can lead the discussion away from where the speaker (not you, the listener) wants it to go. There are several types you can use.

Closed questions

These invite a "Yes" or "No" or other short reply. For example, "Were you at work yesterday?"; answer, "Yes" (or "No"). "What time did you get in?"; answer, "Ten to nine". "Which way did you come in?"; answer, "Side door." And so on.

These quick answers put you under pressure to think of the next question. You soon start to miss replies to your questions and have a really hard time - which you might then blame on the employee. So, be careful with them.

Leading questions

These indicate the expected reply, eg, "Did you enjoy it?" leads to "Yes, thanks", and you now have to find another question. So: be careful with leading questions.

Leading questions can show the assumptions in your mind and may make it seem that you are attacking the person, eg, "You left the key in, didn't you?"

Some may be a waste of time, eg, "You were in at ten to nine, right?"

But they have their uses. The last one could be used to establish common ground and understanding before moving forward.

Open questions

These invite a longer reply, eg, "What happened as you arrived yesterday?"; answer, "Well, I got in about ten to nine, came in through the side door as usual and . . . "

Open questions usually take pressure off you but you may have to ask some further questions, or prompt for clarification, eg, nods, eye contact, "I see", "Hm hm", "Go on", etc. And SILENCE.

Open questions include simple one-worders like "Why?" and "How?"

"What do you think?" gets people thinking and, "Tell me about it" is a lovely way to get people to do just that. However, the employee does need to know what you are talking about when you ask an open question or they'll ask you one back: "What do you mean?"

After an open question you can still use a probing question and, if the person strays off the subject, you can bring them back to it.

Probing Questions

These get the speaker to expand. Probing questions may also be closed questions and can lead to open questions, for example,

"You said you managed several staff; *how many?*"

"Oh, just three."

"I see, *tell me* how you handled them."

By using active listening and good questioning you encourage employees to share problems and ideas. You do this in a way that both increases their confidence and builds on their ability to solve problems.

If you have to work at these skills, and most people do, then you also need to be aware of the forces working against you. Some of these are on the next page.

> *"We exchanged many frank words in our respective languages."*

How you can *interfere* with good listening

10.   Here are several BLOCKS TO GOOD LISTENING.
       Check if any of them ever apply to you.
       If so please mark them.

Blocks to good listening	Tick if it applies to you
a. Rehearsing your reply while the other person is speaking - so you don't hear the rest of his words.	
b. Being hurried, and listening on the run.	
c. Hearing only what you want to hear, and screening out the unwelcome bits.	
d. Other things on your mind, so you can't give your full attention to the speaker.	
e. Disagreeing with the other person's point of view (back to [a] above).	
f. Evaluating what is being said, ie, getting hung up on the early words and not hearing the rest.	
g. Feeling pressured that you must make a decision or have an answer at once (back to [a] above).	
h. Searching for the next question - so that you cannot listen to the last response.	

Most managers mark most of those 'blocks to good listening' so don't feel bad if you marked a few as well. But you should now make a decision.

11.   Of those blocks to good listening that you marked, which *two or three* must you really work on? Please note here how you will overcome them.

```
┌──────────────────────────────────────────────┐
│                                              │
│                                              │
│                                              │
│                                              │
│                                              │
│                                              │
│                                              │
│                                              │
│                                              │
└──────────────────────────────────────────────┘
```

Looking at your own work situation now, what can you say to these questions?

12.   If you have briefing groups when did you last check that people at the bottom know what they ought to know from the latest briefing? If you don't have briefing groups, should you have them?

```
┌──────────────────────────────────────────────┐
│                                              │
│                                              │
│                                              │
└──────────────────────────────────────────────┘
```

13. Do any of your people ever present their views in an unorganised way so that you lose concentration or butt in? If so, how could they be helped to do better?

```
┌──────────────────────────────────────────────┐
│                                              │
│                                              │
│                                              │
│                                              │
└──────────────────────────────────────────────┘
```

14. Have you any people who are not very good at voicing opinions or suggestions?

   Do you ask for their views in a general way, or do you focus your questions on some aspect of the problem where they can show their expertise? Which is better?

15. How would you feel about declaring that participation is your aim, and asking to be challenged if you move away from it?

16. To what extent are you satisfied that the training and development of your people fits them to make a full contribution to discussions?

17. To what extent do your people know the problems:

   a. facing the organisation?

   b. facing their department?

   so that they know where opinions and suggestions are needed?

Ask yourself this

18. If you didn't ask your employees for their opinions and suggestions what would that say to them about your opinion of them?

19. If you didn't ask your employees for their opinions and suggestions how would that affect your own work and results?

Comments

Your responses probably indicated that *not* seeking ideas and suggestions is a mug's game.

Your employees, at the worst, could act as if they had no brains and that would have a very negative effect on you.

And you simply can't do the thinking for everybody - unless you employ robots.

Questions you have been wanting to ask

So far we have been plugging the benefits of "Encourage the employee to express their opinions and make suggestions", but what about the downside? Here are a couple of questions that managers have been known to ask. How would you answer them?

20. "Does this mean that I must always ask for opinions and suggestions before we get to a plan of action? Some of them wouldn't have ideas anyway because the problem is outside their experience."

21. "What if I don't like their opinions and suggestions? They won't be right all the time."

Comments

If people know that you are likely to ask for their opinions and suggestions they are likely to start thinking before you ask. That has to be good. See also Skill Five.

Handling unwelcome ideas can be done in several ways. In all the other books in this series the demonstrations give examples. One book gives specific ways of avoiding the work that often comes when other people say, "Why don't we . . ?"

Practice makes perfect

22. Your work so far in this section suggests several ways of practising this skill. Please look back over the questions, plus your responses and comments, and then circle below those that you want to work on.

1	2	3	4
5	6	7	8
9	10	11	12
13	14	15	16
17	18	19	20

21

23. Consider now which of your people:

    a.   need to be encouraged to speak up more, and

    b.   which of your people bring you problems and who you would like to get into the habit of bringing you solutions as well.

Please note them here.

Finally

"Encourage the employee to express their opinions and make suggestions" is a coaching skill; you can really enjoy practising it - and developing your staff.

It is also at the heart of good time management with your staff, especially when their problems may steal your time.

Notes

WHERE ARE WE NOW?

1. Maintain or enhance the self-esteem of the employee.   √

2. Don't attack the person, FOCUS ON THE PROBLEM.   √

3. Don't assume that the employee has committed an offence.   √

4. Encourage the employee to express their opinions and
    make suggestions.   √

**5. ALLOW THE EMPLOYEE ADEQUATE TIME
    TO THINK THROUGH THE PROBLEM AND
    TO SUGGEST A SOLUTION.**

---

6. Ensure that the employee has an appropriate action programme.

7. Always set a specific follow-up date.

SKILL 5.

ALLOW THE EMPLOYEE ADEQUATE TIME TO THINK THROUGH THE PROBLEM AND TO SUGGEST A SOLUTION.

There is no point in asking people for solutions to problems if they don't have adequate time to think them through; quality solutions take time. "Adequate" could be five seconds or five weeks depending on the problem and the circumstances.

Rushing into a solution that has not been thought through may mean that the problem has to be tackled again in the future. This is like saying, "We don't have time to do it right now but we shall have time to do it all again later."

This skill helps team members to share responsibility for thinking and for the ensuing action. When an employee has thought through the problem and suggested a solution *he* has the clearest mental picture of that solution; this will usually be a better picture than if you tried to communicate your own solution. Moreover, if employees find that their solution needs modifying as they go along, they will be more willing and able to do that.

However, if *you* impose a solution and something goes wrong with it, the employee may return and pressure you for more ideas. And if you had previously thought that the employee lacked initiative this new delay and pressure on you seems to confirm it! But the employee is just reacting to not being given enough time to think things through.

Skills 4 and 5 together are about *genuine* participation. At its lowest level this means that employees have had their say and you have taken their views into account. At its highest level it means that they have been able to fully understand what needs to be achieved and why, they have been able to make some useful contribution, and they can understand why decisions go one way rather than another. They are therefore more committed to the task.

The corollary of allowing the employee adequate thinking time is to allow *yourself* adequate thinking time for a problem, especially in a one-to-one situation, eg, if both of you are stuck be ready to adjourn so you both have more thinking time.

But be careful there. If you are *both* thinking about a problem you must ask: who has responsibility for coming up with the solution? It should usually be the employee.

When the employee suggests a solution you are able to ask the right coaching questions and they have to justify *their* ideas (which they now own) instead of you having to justify yours (which they don't own). And why not? It's a challenge, it develops the people who are your greatest asset, and the solution presented may surprise you with its creativity and originality.

Will you take a couple of minutes to consider some ideas for allowing adequate thinking time? They are in the left-hand column; in the right-hand column will you please give to each idea points out of ten according to the value they have *for you* in your circumstances. Be realistic.

How many points out of ten for allowing adequate thinking time?	Points
1. Pace a discussion so that there is time for the employee to think. Also for you, through your listening and coaching skills, to help the employee to think in a creative and productive manner.	
2. Ensure that people attending meetings have time to think and to speak. This means giving them due notice and information on important matters to be discussed in the meeting.	
3. Realise that *not* allowing adequate time will discourage contributions from employees. This is because they think they are (a) being pressured (into possible errors) or (b) not really expected to have ideas anyway.	

Comments are on the next page.

Comments

The points you awarded to items on the previous page are personal to you but here are the author's comments.

How many points out of ten for allowing adequate thinking time?	Points
1. Pace a discussion so that there is time for the employee to think. Also for you, through your listening and coaching skills, to help the employee to think in a creative and productive manner.	
If communication takes 80% of your time it must pay to get it right first time. Manage your time with your people to achieve this.	
2. Ensure that people attending meetings have time to think and to speak. This means giving them due notice and information on important matters to be discussed in the meeting.	
Ensure that agendas for meetings, with supporting papers, go out in good time so that people can prepare. Meetings should then be shorter but more effective - and cheaper too.	
3. Realise that *not* allowing adequate time will discourage contributions from employees. This is because they think they are (a) being pressured (into possible errors) or (b) not really expected to have ideas anyway.	
If you want to delegate work, plan far enough ahead to be able to do so with reasonable deadlines, not panic situations. If you are not seen to allow enough time you will appear not to want contributions.	

Please take a few more minutes to look at these further ideas and award each one points out of ten according to how they would suit your situation. Be practical.

How many points out of ten for allowing adequate thinking time?	Points
4. Raise problems (including how to handle opportunities) before you have worked out a proposal yourself.	
5. Use the concept of "acceptance time" for change. People need to feel that they had enough time to think through all that could go wrong. Only then will they be ready to switch into positive thinking to solve each problem they have identified.	
6. Be prepared for ideas to be bounced around in a team before the best solution emerges - and allow time for this to happen. In any team some people may have flashes of inspiration which need other people to develop them. Building on ideas and/or developing alternatives takes time but it's good and necessary teamwork.	
7. Accept that you cannot do the thinking for your employees, not even for one of them. If you try you will not be doing your own job properly. This is coaching them to think of their own ideas.	

Comments are on the next two pages.

Comments

How many points out of ten for allowing adequate thinking time?	Points
4. Raise problems (including how to handle opportunities) before you have worked out a proposal yourself.	
Doing this gets contributions from your team *before* you are too attached to your own ideas, and those contributions will be wider ranging. You must still adopt the best solution but now have more options. Ideas from well-trained people should be more practicable and, of course, will be owned by them. This also allows more time for you to be doing what only you can do.	
5. Use the concept of "acceptance time" for change. People need to feel that they had enough time to think through all that could go wrong. Only then will they be ready to switch into positive thinking to solve each problem they have identified.	
If you allow enough time for thinking you don't have to push for action before people are ready to "give it a go". Genuine participation again.	
6. Be prepared for ideas to be bounced around in a team before the best solution emerges - and allow time for this to happen. In any team some people may have flashes of inspiration which need other people to develop them. Building on ideas and/or developing alternatives takes time but it's good and necessary teamwork.	
If you allow time for a bit of "brainstorming" you may get many ideas but nothing that is quite right. But you are then in a strong position to combine bits from various alternatives to come up with a best solution which achieves what you want and which is not a compromise.	

Comments (Continued)

How many points out of ten for allowing adequate thinking time?	Points
7. Accept that you cannot do the thinking for your employees, not even for one of them. If you try you will not be doing your own job properly. This is coaching them to think of their own ideas.	

If you try to do the thinking for your people you will not be developing them. In fact, you will be over-loading yourself *and* holding them up as well. That will never get you promoted.

After these comments, and reflecting on your own responses, would you want to go back and change any of the values you awarded on the previous pages - thinking about practical value in your own situation?

Now use the following questions to focus on your own working practices and to decide if you want to make any changes to them.

8. Looking at your current practice, where would you place yourself between the two extremes on this scale?

Stopping your people thinking for themselves by *giving* them solutions to problems.

Encouraging them to devise their own solutions (but for your approval).

Please mark one of the boxes.

9. Where do you usually stand on planning? Please mark your position on the scale below.

Do you some-
times leave things
until they become
urgent, then pass
on your panic
situations to
others?

Do you usually
estimate the
resources for a
job, especially
time, and then
follow your
plan?

10. To what extent do your people have conceptual frameworks to help them to think through problems and present proposals in a form which helps you to make a decision? (Circle one please.)

Greatly?   Moderately?   Not at all?

11. Asking people for ideas but not allowing them enough time to think through the problem is called *pseudo*-participation, ie, "consultation" occurs but with not enough time for a quality solution to emerge. If you do this at all how can you correct it?

12. One test of your ability to "Allow the employee adequate time . . ." is: to what extent do your people come up with solutions to problems? (Circle one.)

Greatly?   Moderately?   Not at all?

Ask yourself this

Both this skill, "Allow the employee adequate time to think through the problem and to suggest a solution", and Skill No. 4, "Encourage the employee to express their opinions and make suggestions", are about *coaching*.

Coaching is a combination of skills which can give you increased *leverage*. Increasing your leverage means that, by better use of your people, you achieve more in the time available to you. Raising your level of achievement makes you more eligible for promotion (or for greater returns if you are the head guy already). Or you can spend more time with your family.

13. If coaching gives you more leverage, and if that is something you want, what obstacles stand in the way of you going for it?

```
┌──────────────────────────────────────────┐
│                                            │
│                                            │
│                                            │
│                                            │
└──────────────────────────────────────────┘
```

14. If you don't increase your leverage through coaching what other means do you have?

```
┌──────────────────────────────────────────┐
│                                            │
│                                            │
│                                            │
│                                            │
└──────────────────────────────────────────┘
```

15. If you don't increase your leverage one way or another how will that affect your career?

```
┌──────────────────────────────────────────┐
│                                            │
│                                            │
│                                            │
│                                            │
└──────────────────────────────────────────┘
```

Questions you have been wanting to ask

What many managers say, of course, is, "This coaching idea is all very well but I just don't have the time to wait for an employee to learn about something and then come with an answer to a problem."

Fair enough. If an employee doesn't know how to handle a problem and you do, then tell him and save both of you a lot of time, especially when they are new to the job. Yes?

Well, if you tell the employee the solution the task gets done. But would you prefer the employee to know *why* the solution is appropriate? Of course you would, because another problem will come along that is similar but not identical, when the employee won't have you on hand to give instructions.

So, sometimes, instead of quickly giving a solution why not ask a few questions that will get the employee *thinking through the problem* and thus towards a solution. These are the types of questions mentioned under Skill No. 2 and in No. 4.

Or, you can ask the employee what options they can think of for a solution. Most times you will hear two or more choices for you to approve one of them, or a mixture. For each option you can ask "Why?" At this point you will hear the employee's thinking and you can improve the thought processes, if necessary, with further questions.

Or, you could offer the employee two or three options for a solution and ask which they prefer. Then back to "Why?" and other questions, eg, "If you do that how would it affect the (other product or component, or whatever)?"

Allowing the employee adequate time now - and a few questions won't take long - means that they *learn*, which will save time for both of you in the future. In addition, you are learning about the employee and how far you can trust their thinking. Contrast that with just giving instructions.

And, in any case, what about when you *don't* have an answer, when you are as much in the dark as the employee? The employee is always closest to the job and, quite probably, the expert. Your coaching questions help them to think through the problem and to suggest a solution. Also, *they* are doing the really hard work - thinking.

What managers also ask is, "What do I do if they come up with solutions that are wrong? Don't I risk knocking their self-esteem if this happens often?"

16. So what do you think? Please write your answer in the box below. You should know, however, that you have read the answer already.

Comments

Is there anything in the previous page that would help? Read it again if necessary.

How would you feel about asking the employee for another option if you don't like their first idea? You could let the bad ideas just fall away.

How would you feel about the, "If you do that how would it affect the . . . ?" type of question, perhaps as a lead-in to asking for another option?

People learn from mistakes so it's better that they make them at the stage of *proposing* a solution rather than executing one (although that may still happen). Coaching questions give insight to mistakes so let your people know that this is your style.

Incidentally, "Credit where it's due", which is another book in this series, gives ideas that you can use to help employees think through problems and suggest solutions.

Practice makes perfect

17. There are quite a few ideas in this section to encourage you to "Allow the employee adequate time to think through the problem and to suggest a solution". Will you please check your responses to the questions listed below and then circle those that you want to work on.

1	2	3	4
5	6	7	8
9	10	11	12
13	14	15	16

Now you can look back to Skill Number Four and, if you noted there someone who you wanted to bring you solutions instead of problems, note them below. Then note whether you will be *asking* them for options or *offering* them options with, in both cases, back-up questions to get their thinking.

Finally

Thinking is the hardest work there is so don't feel bad about delegating it. Besides it helps to develop character in people.

A coaching session may take two minutes; the employee then gets to work - and you can get on with your own job.

Also, this way, you can be in the happy position of approving the employee's ideas rather than having them finding fault with yours.

If you do go in for brainstorming (Q6), ensure you get all ideas noted *before* they are evaluated. Otherwise you'll get bogged down with arguments over the first idea.

WHERE ARE WE NOW?

1. Maintain or enhance the self-esteem of the employee. √

2. Don't attack the person, FOCUS ON THE PROBLEM. √

3. Don't assume that the employee has committed an offence. √

4. Encourage the employee to express their opinions and make suggestions. √

5. Allow the employee adequate time to think through the problem and to suggest a solution. √

6. ENSURE THAT THE EMPLOYEE HAS AN APPROPRIATE ACTION PROGRAMME.

7. Always set a specific follow-up date.

SKILL 6.

ENSURE THAT THE EMPLOYEE HAS AN APPROPRIATE ACTION PROGRAMME.

When all is said and done, there's a lot more said than done. We have all heard people saying, "Okay, let's do that" without agreeing who, specifically, will do what - and no one does anything.

If the previous skills in this framework have been well applied this one wraps up the action resulting from the ideas discussed. If you listened well you will have assessed the employee's thinking and commitment, and will be more confident in the action programme which, because the employee contributed to it, is more likely to be appropriate.

As the leader of your team you are accountable for its results and how they are obtained so "appropriate" means appropriate in *your* view.

Think of a "programme" as a series of steps with a time scale, or just a single step - as appropriate. For some action plans it is useful to ask the employee to *summarise* so you can check his or her understanding. This can be really useful when working in the larger team so that everyone understands what everyone else is doing.

The summary may be detailed and explicit the first time an employee does a new task or where the employee is junior. On the other hand, if an employee knows a task well, appropriate action may be implicit: "Leave it with me, I'll fix it." A senior or specialist team member may simply be left to get on with it and, as an expert, works things out.

Sometimes it may be appropriate for the employee to do nothing, but *not* if the boss is then doing the employee's work. Sometimes the action may be to give the problem more thought and come back with ideas. Whichever, you also should be clear about what you will do - if anything.

Ensure that the employee *has* the programme, ie that they understand it. Telling the employee what to do may mean that you "passed the ball" but it does not mean that he "took possession" of it.

People cannot develop if you are not prepared to take a risk on them doing something new (the next skill will help to handle the risk), and sometimes an action programme that you all thought was "appropriate" will turn out to be wrong.

However, if your problem analysis and decision making was done as well as possible, that action plan would have seemed the best thing *at the time*, and you can't do better than that. You have to accept that failures will happen from time to time, that you have done your best to avoid or reduce them, and that you - and your people - are prepared to learn from them.

Another reason for using this skill is that employees should be clear about the standards of performance expected of them and the goals they are working towards.

Of the following items which would cause an action programme to be MORE appropriate, and which LESS appropriate? Please tick. Comments are on the next page.

More appropriate or less appropriate?	More	Less
1. Hearing, assessing, amending (if necessary) and approving *their* ideas.		
2. Keeping discussions on track so that employees' contributions are appropriate.		
3. Hearing action steps summarised (by them and not by you) except in very simple situations.		
4. Letting employees know where you (and organisation policy) stand on an issue so that their ideas can take this into account.		

Comments

Which of the following items would cause an action
programme to be more appropriate, and which less so?

More appropriate or less appropriate?	More	Less
1. Hearing, assessing, amending (if necessary) and approving *their* ideas.	✓	
Yes, there it is again, we said this at the end of Skill No. 5. You know how people, quite legitimately, question your ideas when you put them forward? Getting their ideas is far more comfortable.		
2. Keeping discussions on track so that employees' contributions are appropriate.	✓	
But you should still allow for a little 'serendipity', that is, for fruitful if digressive discussion.		
3. Hearing action steps summarised (by them and not by you) except in very simple situations.	✓	
When you hear them summarise you get the picture they have in *their* minds, you already know what is in your own. You can correct things if their picture doesn't accord with yours.		
4. Letting employees know where you (and organisation policy) stand on an issue so that their ideas can take this into account.	✓	
This is the right thing in most day-to-day discussions; then you don't have to cut the ground from under their feet when they come up with ideas which conflict with your position.		

Here are more questions in similar vein. Of the following items which would cause an action programme to be more appropriate, and which less appropriate? Please tick.

More appropriate or less appropriate?	More	Less
5. Giving *direction* without necessarily giving instructions, ie, giving the "what must be achieved" rather than "how it must be done".		
6. Taking notes where sensible. Writing down the programme where information needs to be shared; using the document as a checklist.		
7. Checking that the agreed action advances the team towards desired results, even if the action plan is sometimes no more than to think up some ideas.		
8. Building in opportunities for employees to develop and learn new skills from what they do.		
9. Giving more weight to those employees with greater seniority or longer experience.		
10. Getting decisions based on logic and reasoned argument, rather than on rank or loudness.		

Comments are on the next two pages.

Comments

More appropriate or less appropriate?	More	Less
5. Giving *direction* without necessarily giving instructions, ie, giving the "what must be achieved" rather than "how it must be done".	✓	
Then listening to ideas, pulling them together and finally *agreeing* "how it will be done" so that everyone is clear. A new and inexperienced employee may need to be told more of the "how to do it" but should later be able to work things out for him/herself.		
6. Taking notes where sensible. Writing down the programme where information needs to be shared; using the document as a checklist.	✓	
Notes can be kept simple, just key words. Sharing a written programme means everyone is "singing from the same hymn sheet".		
7. Checking that the agreed action advances the team towards desired results, even if the action plan is sometimes no more than to think up some ideas.	✓	
The action programme, not surprisingly, should take you towards where you want to be. The thinking may be in order to clarify where you want to be. In other words, until desired results are clear to all concerned any plan to get there may take you somewhere else.		

Comments (Continued)

More appropriate or less appropriate?	More	Less
8. Building in opportunities for employees to develop and learn new skills from what they do.	✓	
If you are in a changing business you *need* to be testing out new ways of handling things (Skill 7 helps to reduce the risk involved in this). Always be on the lookout for opportunities to develop your staff - and yourself.		
9. Giving more weight to those employees with greater seniority or longer experience.		✓
This is the odd one out. Generally speaking, people with greater seniority and/or experience may be expected to produce better arguments to support ideas. And their doubts may be better founded. But you can't afford to bank on it. Ideas and doubts need to be tested against what an action plan is required to achieve; the criteria for success.		
10. Getting decisions based on logic and reasoned argument, rather than on rank or loudness.	✓	
You are looking for *what* is right rather than *who* is right. This takes us back once again to good problem analysis and decision-making that we mentioned earlier in Skill 2.		

Now let's move nearer to your own work situation.

Computer software programmes can be useful for planning even quite small projects. They can provide flow charts and help with time management so that people avoid overload.

11. Can you name just one such programme? There is quite a large range.

Action plans are often decided within meetings and then *some* people will still wait for the minutes to come out before they take action.

12. If you were to check on meetings which you attended over, say, the past three months, and which produced minutes, what do you think you would find, generally speaking? Circle one please.

Minutes are produced, generally speaking:

within two working days

half-way between meetings

just before the next meeting.

Comments

11. There are Personal Information Managers (PIMs) by, eg, Corel Wordperfect, Lotus, Microsoft and many others. If you don't have anything for personal use, or for project management, you only need to ask around for something that suits *you*.

12. The next question is, do you need to be working towards an improvement?

You may have someone who is sometimes not as detailed in their thinking as they could be. They promise to do something without thinking of all the steps, and thus the time required. Result? They start the job too late and overrun.

Coaching questions can help them to work up a better action plan. For example, "I must plan ahead" sounds good and, with some employees, it would be enough. With another you may ask, "How will you *ensure* you plan ahead?", earning the reply, "I'll write down all the steps I need to take."

If you need to tighten it up further you may then ask "Fine, how about the time side of it?" Reply, "Yes, I'll have to estimate each step, and work backwards to a start date."

And so it goes. Coaching is a continuous process about different things with different people at different stages of their development.

13. Do you have any people who would benefit from coaching questions to tighten up action programmes?

What about larger meetings where you are not the chairman but an ordinary member? You may have been in such a meeting when action plans developed were not appropriate because people had skirted or not identified the real issues.

14. How could you affect that through good use of Skill No. 2, "Don't attack the person, **focus on the problem**"? Comments are on the next page.

Comments

It can be useful to recap the problem as you understand it and then ask how the plan will help with some aspect(s) of the problem. Or a variation on this. You need to use open questions because closed ones could get you short and unhelpful replies.

Probably a better way is to come in rather sooner and make a contribution at the problem analysis stage. Failing that, try to have more *options* generated later when a solution is being sought. Combining parts from different options can also bring a better solution, eg, "Yes, and if we do that it will fix the other problem as well."

Ask yourself this

15. Do you have any employees with whom you exercise tight supervision because you fear mistakes or mis-understandings? If so, how would the guidance for this skill be useful?

16. Have you ever found yourself doing work which should really have been taken on by an employee? If so, does this happen with any employee(s) in particular? Who? And how should you change things?

17. When employees do something which is new to them this is an opportunity for them to develop. How do you feel about *actively* seeking opportunities for new work like this?

Questions you have been wanting to ask

18. "What do I do if they don't do what they promised to do? And keep on not doing what they've promised to do? And I've coached them until I'm blue in the face?"

    Go on, then, have a go. What *do* you do?

Comments

This situation can cause stress because, if you deal with people in the wrong way, you could be on the losing side at an industrial tribunal.

There are no easy answers because managers often face complex situations. However, other books in this series are relevant. These cover how to change performance which is unacceptable, how to overcome resistance to change, and how to go about using discipline if you have to. These are important areas which cannot be covered in this book.

19. "What do I do with a person who wants to do only interesting, creative things? The job has changed and they need to change." An example is a Web designer who creates a large web site but is weak on the chores connected with maintenance.

What *do* you do?

Comments

Jobs change and many people have to change careers, even relatively late in life. If someone wants to carry on doing what they are doing, and that work is not available with you, they are free to look elsewhere or set up on their own. Consider an aptitude test? Or redundancy?

20. "Can I never just give a straight instruction?"

Comments

You said, "Of course I can." To say anything else would be ridiculous. Imagine calling one of your people and saying, "What do I want you to do?"

Coaching isn't everything. It's just one in a range of management tools and techniques.

Practice makes perfect

21. This skill is all about making the right things happen so will you please review what has been said, by you and by the author, and then circle below those questions that you want to work on.

1	2	3	4
5	6	7	8
9	10	11	12
13	14	15	16
17	18	19	20

Finally

Before you break away from a deliberate, work-centred discussion you should check yourself through all seven Practical Leadership Skills, but this one, No. 6, "Ensure that the employee has an appropriate action programme", does need really careful thought.

Does the employee *have* the programme, ie, do they understand it and accept it?

Have they contributed to it; so that their understanding and acceptance is better?

Is it appropriate, ie, will it deal with the situation?

If it is at all complicated have you heard them summarise it?

Remember,   "When all is said and done, there's a lot more said than done." Don't let that apply to you.

Notes

WHERE ARE WE NOW?

1. Maintain or enhance the self-esteem of the employee. √

2. Don't attack the person, FOCUS ON THE PROBLEM. √

3. Don't assume that the employee has committed an offence. √

4. Encourage the employee to express their opinions and make suggestions. √

5. Allow the employee adequate time to think through the problem and to suggest a solution. √

6. Ensure that the employee has an appropriate action programme. √

---

7. ALWAYS SET A SPECIFIC FOLLOW-UP DATE.

SKILL 7.

ALWAYS SET A SPECIFIC FOLLOW-UP DATE.

A follow-up date sets a deadline. Without this, and with the best will in the world, other things may become more urgent. It allows time for things to be done right; but if you see something going badly wrong you can intervene before the date if you wish.

Together with Skill 6, the follow-up date helps the employee in planning and setting priorities. Because you *both* agree the follow-up date you are able to insist that it be met - or deferred only for good reason. You thus have control but, with this and the other skills, you also have participation!

It can *reduce risk* during some new venture: by having an action plan in small stages and having the employee report after each one. It can *show trust* in an employee: by extending the period before the next report-back. It can *help people to develop and learn,* eg, an employee can be coached through stages of something new with each follow-up date bringing a review, praise and then the plan for the next stage.

If you are using the delegation process you might progress from very tight follow-ups for the first time a task is done, through to "Let me know if there's anything you can't handle", (a specific event where the employee takes the initiative) after handing over the task completely.

Often a follow-up date will be used for a review in order to improve; to discuss what went well with a plan and why, what went wrong and why, are we still going in the right direction, and so on.

Setting a follow-up date indicates that you think something is sufficiently important for you to follow it through; not setting a follow-up date indicates that you probably won't be following up and that has to have an effect on people.

Setting a follow-up date helps to close discussion on a topic and move on. It may be specific in diary terms ("9 a.m. on the 23rd") or specific in event terms ("Let me know if you fall behind plan").

Don't confuse following up with the action plan in Skill 6. The follow-up is to *check* what happened with the action plan, to see that you are achieving what you set out to achieve, that you are indeed advancing towards your goal. And you should get the employee reporting to you, rather than you having to chase them.

Should we *always* set a specific follow-up date? Remember that we are looking here at deliberate work-centred discussions and a follow-up date is a motivator. It can be as simple as looking at a diary list, asking, "Did this happen?" and crossing off one more item.

As with all of the other skills, you use this one as you think fit; it is for you to *decide* whether you need to set a specific follow-up date. If setting it is a motivator, then being seen to write it down has to be even better.

1. Here are four examples of a manager setting a follow-up date. Please rank them from 1, for the best, to 4 for the worst, in terms of overall value/effectiveness.

	Four ways of setting a specific follow-up date	Your ranking
a.	"I'll be round nine o'clock Thursday to see how it's going."	
b.	"I'll be round at nine o'clock Thursday to check up on you."	
c.	"We'll look at it again next week."	
d.	"When can you come back to me on this?"	

Comments are on the next page.

Comments

	Four ways of setting a specific follow-up date	Your ranking
a.	"I'll be round nine o'clock Thursday to see how it's going."	2
	That seems to be friendly enough, non-threatening, but precise. Something you can note in your diary or to-do list. This may mean just the same as (b).	
b.	"I'll be round at nine o'clock Thursday to check up on you."	4
	But (a) is far more acceptable. Few managers would use (b), it's too distrustful, but at least the employee knows where he stands. Which is more than can be said for the next way of setting a follow-up date.	
c.	"We'll look at it again next week."	3
	This can mean any time between Sunday and Saturday. Being hard to enter in your diary this can lead to misunderstandings when your employee expects you to raise the matter at the end of the week, and you roll up on Wednesday. It can also send the wrong message to your employee; that you hope the problem will just go away and you are not going to check up at all.	
d.	"When can you come back to me on this?"	1
	This asks the employee to plan the work in with their other priorities. This should generate more commitment and, if you really, *really* have to, you can change the employee's priorities if this task, in your view, warrants it.	

"Often a follow-up date will be used for a review in order to improve". Let's take that a little further, because if you want to take advantage of opportunities for learning it's good to have a framework for doing so.

2. Do you want your people (and yourself) to learn both from successes and from mistakes? Circle one please.

Yes   No

3. Would you like the learning from one situation to be applied to other current and future projects, processes and procedures? Circle one please.

Yes   No

4. In reviewing how an action programme has worked out which should you discuss first?

The successes?   The mistakes?

Will you explain your choice please?

5. One way or another you are probably reviewing things in your mind for much of the time. How useful would it be to log ideas for learning (or insights) in order to discuss them in upcoming meetings? Circle one.

Very useful?   Pretty useful?

Barely useful?   No use at all?

Comments are on the next page.

Comments

2.	Do you want your people (and yourself) to learn both from successes and from mistakes?

That's a leading question if ever there was one. But it's here because if you want learning to happen you have to decide, as now, to make it happen.

3.	Would you like the learning from one situation to be applied to other current and future projects, processes and procedures? Circle one please.

Well, of course you would. But this means that you have to ask questions like, "Where else can we use this right now?" And, "*Who* else could use this?"

The thought of rewriting processes or procedures may act as a deterrent to applying new learning. This is a good argument for keeping them as simple as possible so that changes can be made more easily.

4.	In reviewing how an action programme has worked out which should you discuss first? And why?

Successes every time. Building on positive things is good for self-esteem all round. Then, after discussing areas for improvement, you can close with a reminder of the successes.
  NB: "Areas for improvement", not mistakes.

5.	You probably review things in your mind quite often. How useful would it be to note pieces of learning for discussion in upcoming meetings?

If you don't write them down you might forget them. You could also ask your people to log and share their learning. This helps to build a culture of *deliberate* learning from *real experience* - often the best teacher of all. Try to learn from small lessons so that you don't learn, too late, from big nasty ones.

How long might a review take? And how should we actually go about reviewing in order to improve? Let's look for answers to those two questions.

6.   When you come to a follow-up date with an individual employee, where a review in order to improve *could be worthwhile*, how long might that review take?

7.   And, with an individual, how would you actually go about reviewing in order to improve? Specifically, what one or two questions would you ask? Please note them here.

8.   How would you handle a review differently if you were with the whole team?

Comments are on the next page.

Comments

6.	When you come to a follow-up date with an individual employee, where a review in order to improve *could be worthwhile*, how long might that review take?

After you have listened to the employee telling you about the task or whatever, how long does it take to say, "Fine, what can we learn from . . . (the doing of it, or some part of it that went well, or some part that went not so well)?

Whatever time you take should be time well spent.

7.	And, with an individual, how would you actually go about reviewing in order to improve? Specifically, what one or two questions would you ask?

No. 6 above gave a nice open question which will probably be enough on most occasions. If you want to be more structured you might ask (a) "*What* went well?" and, maybe, "*Why* did it go well?" (b) "How can we avoid (that problem) in future?" or "Where do we need to improve?"

You can see how these questions allow the employee to mention the role of others in the team.

8.	How would you handle a review differently if you were with the whole team?

Before you even get to a review you may wish to establish the *idea* of reviews, that they will not be used to find scapegoats but for learning. That when people do new things they can expect mistakes (which become areas for improvement). That they should expect the unexpected - and learn from it. That they should seek to learn, eg, why a previously successful practice didn't work this time.

You will probably be more structured with a group and ensure that you seek opinions from each in turn, and suggestions too.

Looking now at your own work situation and how you work with colleagues as well as with your staff:

9.   Are any of your colleagues sometimes content *not* to set a follow-up date - with resulting problems? If so, how could you improve the situation?

```



```

10. In your experience what are people likely to think if you don't set a follow-up date for something?

```



```

11. Sometimes people agree a follow-up date which allows insufficient time for the task to be done properly. This leads to pressure and sometimes to failure.

     Do you ever agree to follow-up dates, for yourself or for your team, which are too tight? If so, how can you avoid doing that?

```



```

12. Do any of your team set themselves deadlines which *you* believe to be too tight - and you turn out to be correct? If so, what should you do about that?

13. Let's look in a different direction for a moment. Do you, when you are dealing with your own boss, ever let them get away without agreeing a follow-up date? If so what can you do in that sort of situation?

Comments are below for questions 12 and 13.

12. You probably said something about asking questions: about workload, about the parts of the task and how long each will take. About how much time they should allow for the unexpected, and so on.

13. Very likely you will have had experience of setting a follow-up date for yourself and pursuing your boss when it comes round. Bosses are like anyone else; if they realise something is important to you they are more likely to respond. And will it hurt if you are seen to be keen and determined?

Questions you have been wanting to ask

Have a go at these before you look at the comments.

14. "What if they don't do what they have promised?"

```



```

15. "What if they want to defer a follow-up date?

```



```

16. "What if I can't keep to a follow-up date?

```



```

Comments are on the next page.

Comments

---

14. "What if they don't do what they have promised?"

If you are known to expect people to stick to follow-up dates that reduces the possibility of failure - for whatever reason.

Otherwise you may need to look at your coaching, they may have to look at their time management. Certainly you should not continue to allow commitments to be missed.

In extreme cases, and if you need help, you may want to look at the book in this series which deals specifically with changing unacceptable performance.

---

15. "What if they want to defer a follow-up date?

You should really not allow this. Get the employee to come to you with whatever they've got. After all, you planned your time so that you would have, say, two to five minutes for coaching and you need the chance to assess and develop the employee.

Let them off the meeting and (in an extreme case) the employee will have done nothing. Insist that they come and report and, by the time they get to your office, they will have something to show. Moreover, they will do better next time.

Planned time with your staff is important to you. Five minutes of your time, that short coaching session, will very likely set up your employee for hours of work. That is how *you* get things done.

---

16. "What if I can't keep to a follow-up date?

That is going to be unavoidable at times and your choice is to let your follow-up fade away, or to rearrange it. The former will leave a disillusioned and demotivated employee. The latter will have the opposite effect.

---

17. "Where can we expect to find worthwhile learning opportunities?"

That's a good question and you may already have taken advantage of quite a few learning opportunities when they came along, so why not list them here so that (a) you can pass them on to others when appropriate, and (b) so that you will be just as alert when they come along in future.

As you do that you may, with the benefit of 20/20 hindsight, now realise that there were other opportunities that you did not take at the time. Never mind, list those as well and tick them off in the second column; this is all part of continual learning.

Learning opportunities encountered	Have already taken advantage	Recognise with benefit of hindsight

Comments are on the next page.

Comments

17. You will certainly have noted some of these and you can insert your ticks again if you wish. Plus, there is space to write in your own opportunities, where different, if you want to have them all one one page.

Learning opportunities	Have already taken advantage	Recognise with benefit of hindsight
A job change		
New responsibility		
New work relationships (peers)		
New employees		
A new boss		
A new project		
A new project team		
A performance review (appraisal)		
A seminar or course		
A new task		

Practice makes perfect

You have seen how setting a follow-up date can work well for you in many different ways, and some are listed below.

18. Will you please consider each one and then, where you can, match as many ways as possible to one or more people. Enter their names or initials below (write "all" if you wish). Also, see what other ways you can think of and enter those in the same way.

How a follow-up date can work for you	With whom will you use these ways?
Setting a deadline	
Arranging priorities	
Obtaining participation	
Reducing risk	
Showing trust	
Helping people develop through coaching	
Praising people	
Planning the next stage	

More on the next page.

Matching ways to people, continued.

How a follow-up date can work for you	With whom will you use these ways?
Delegating a new task	
Reviewing in order to improve	
Showing that something is important	
Closing a discussion	
Moving to a new topic	
Checking on progress	
Motivating people	
Getting your boss's help	
Your own way:	
And another:	

Before moving on will you please review the earlier questions in this section, with your responses, and ring the numbers below where you want to follow through.

1	2	3	4
5	6	7	8
9	10	11	12
13	14	15	16
17	18		

Finally

At the end of every work-centred discussion you have to ask yourself,

"Do I (we) need to see what happens with this plan?",

> or

"Do I hope to congratulate someone for doing well?"

> or

"Do we need to see what we can learn from this one?"

> or

a similar sort of question.

Or are you prepared to let things be? It's your decision. If you want to follow up, get a specific date agreed, stick to it and expect your people to do the same.

> "Do I hope it will happen? Or do I want to **make sure** it happens?"

Notes

I can get my people to use email to report progress. But it's not so good (a) for coaching on the next step, nor (b) for asking questions about what they've learned. Unless . . .

WHERE ARE WE NOW?

1. Maintain or enhance the self-esteem of the employee.   √

2. Don't attack the person, FOCUS ON THE PROBLEM.   √

3. Don't assume that the employee has committed an offence.   √

4. Encourage the employee to express their opinions and make suggestions.   √

5. Allow the employee adequate time to think through the problem and to suggest a solution. √

6. Ensure that the employee has an appropriate action programme.   √

7. Always set a specific follow-up date.   √

MORE ABOUT TEAMS	Having already seen several references to teamwork you won't be surprised to find more about teams in this section.

THE LEADER'S RESPONSIBILITIES

This section shows how the seven Practical Leadership Skills are relevant to good teamwork.

When people talk about "teams" they often have in mind perhaps four to eight people. But the smallest team is you and one other person, you and an employee. You will have meetings of the full team but, in your day-to-day work, you probably deal more often with your people as individuals.

If you also lead other teams, eg, committees or project teams, you will often work with their members on a one-to-one basis outside regular meetings.

The Practical Leadership Skills which you use with one person are also used with people in meetings, especially when you realise that in groups you frequently focus on, and work with, the different members in turn.

Much is now known about how teams work and how critical is the role of the team leader. As a team leader, your responsibilities can be broadly split into four areas:[1]

- CLARIFYING the team's goals (immediate, short term and long term) (also called objectives, targets, or standards).

- ADVANCING the team towards those goals, through the way you lead..

- RECOGNISING the different abilities and contributions of team members.

- SHARING with them responsibility for achieving the team's goals - for which you are accountable to your organisation.

We now move on to look at teams of two or more and, using the questions and comments on the next few pages, you can see how the seven Practical Leadership Skills fit in with the above four areas - and other writings on teams.

---

[1] These four key areas of leadership are taken, with thanks and with her permission, from an M.A. thesis by Dr Pat Hedges.

1.   Here again are the seven, all-the-time, Practical
      Leadership Skills:

1.   Maintain or enhance the self-esteem of the employee.
2.   Don't attack the person, FOCUS ON THE PROBLEM.
3.   Don't assume that the employee has committed an offence.
4.   Encourage the employee to express their opinions and make
      suggestions.
5.   Allow the employee adequate time to think through the
      problem and to suggest a solution.
6.   Ensure that the employee has an appropriate action
      programme.
7.   Always set a specific follow-up date.

And here is a checklist for the team leader's first skills area
from the previous page. Please see which of the Practical
Leadership Skills above are reflected in the checklist items
below and mark them off. The first has been done for you.

CLARIFYING the team's goals	Which of the seven skills from above?						
	1	2	3	4	5	6	7
Give the team a clear direction and purpose.	●	●				●	●
Set realistic targets and standards.							
Supply criteria for performance.							
Let them know how all are doing and how this fits into the overall picture of the organisation.							
Ensure that everything you do follows from your organisation's objectives and that this is reflected in the team's objectives.							
Show excitement about the work, a proper sense of urgency and expectations of high standards. (If people see that you are committed they are more likely to be too.)							

Comments are overleaf.

Comments

1. Please check these against those which you marked. You may have all of these or more. You can see that the seven Practical Leadership Skills are used in all sorts of discussions and management practices. They are indeed "all-the-time" skills.

CLARIFYING the team's goals	Which of the seven skills from above?						
	1	2	3	4	5	6	7
Give the team a clear direction and purpose.	●	●				●	●
Set realistic targets and standards.	●	●		●	●	●	●
Supply criteria for performance.	●					●	●
Let them know how all are doing and how this fits into the overall picture of the organisation.	●		●	●			
Ensure that everything you do follows from your organisation's objectives and that this is reflected in the team's objectives.	●	●			●	●	
Show excitement about the work, a proper sense of urgency and expectations of high standards. (If people see that you are committed they are more likely to be too.)	●		●				●

If you wonder why this author marked some of these items but you didn't then look back to the Practical Leadership Skill involved, read the introduction to that section and/or scan the questions and comments. You should find the answers there. If you marked more, that's okay.

The framework of Practical Leadership Skills is, remember, a *framework* for you to flesh out as you wish, and to use as you wish. You may have found connections which this author has missed.

2. Here is the framework of all-the-time skills again:

---

1. Maintain or enhance the self-esteem of the employee.
2. Don't attack the person,
    FOCUS ON THE PROBLEM.
3. Don't assume that the employee has committed an offence.
4. Encourage the employee to express their opinions and make suggestions.
5. Allow the employee adequate time to think through the problem and to suggest a solution.
6. Ensure that the employee has an appropriate action programme.
7. Always set a specific follow-up date.

And here is the team leader's second skills checklist. Please consider which of the Practical Leadership Skills is reflected in that checklist and mark them off.

ADVANCING the team towards its goals	Which of the seven Practical Leadership Skills from above?						
	1	2	3	4	5	6	7
Ensure everyone knows they are working for team and organisation goals, and not for themselves alone.							
Ensure that systems are fair.							
Delegate work whenever possible.							
Appraise, counsel and train others.							
Allocate 'perks' fairly.							

Comments are on the next page.

Comments

2. Again, please check your choices against the author's.

ADVANCING the team towards its goals	Which of the seven Practical Leadership Skills from above?						
	1	2	3	4	5	6	7
Ensure everyone knows they are working for team and organisation goals, and not for themselves alone.			●			●	
Ensure that systems are fair.	●			●			
Delegate work whenever possible.	●	●	●	●	●	●	●
Appraise, counsel and train others.	●	●	●	●	●	●	●
Allocate 'perks' fairly.	●			●			

There are only two of the Practical Leadership Skills marked for the last item but if perquisites are badly allocated you can have a real problem. People will tend to drag their feet if they feel badly done to. They may also feel disinclined to support other team members who they perceive to be better off than they are.

The same applies with systems. For example, you may have a situation in which higher-paid people can cause problems, inadvertently to be sure, for lesser-paid ones who may resent having to put things right.

Delegating? Well, the team won't advance towards its goals if you try to do too much of the work yourself.

3.   Here are those seven Practical Leadership Skills again:

---

1.   Maintain or enhance the self-esteem of the employee.
2.   Don't attack the person,
                    FOCUS ON THE PROBLEM.
3.   Don't assume that the employee has committed an offence.
4.   Encourage the employee to express their opinions and make suggestions.
5.   Allow the employee adequate time to think through the problem and to suggest a solution.
6.   Ensure that the employee has an appropriate action programme.
7.   Always set a specific follow-up date.

And the third checklist is below. Which of the seven Practical Leadership Skills above are reflected in this list? Please mark them off as before.

RECOGNISING the different abilities of team members	Which of the seven Practical Leadership Skills?						
	1	2	3	4	5	6	7
Foster an environment in which people are aware of their strengths and weaknesses.							
Build on the team's strengths and look for ways of improving in the weaker ones.							
Counsel people constructively if you can see ways in which their credibility, respect and trust for others can be improved. Take advice yourself on this point.							

Just three in that checklist. If you can think of more, why not note them in the margin?

Comments are on the next page.

Comments

3. Recognising can have its pleasant side and its more
    awkward side. Either way it is important.

RECOGNISING the different abilities of team members	Which of the seven Practical Leadership Skills?						
	1	2	3	4	5	6	7
Foster an environment in which people are aware of their strengths and weaknesses.	●	●	●	●	●	●	●
Build on the team's strengths and look for ways of improving in the weaker ones.	●	●	●	●	●	●	●
Counsel people constructively if you can see ways in which their credibility, respect and trust for others can be improved. Take advice yourself on this point.	●	●	●	●	●	●	●

Three "full houses", how about that?

We have already covered, in Practical Leadership Skill
No. 7, the idea of using that step to see what can be learned,
ie, reviewing in order to improve.

For the second item, it makes sense for people to do more
of what they are good at. Remember also what was said
back in Skill No. 3, "Don't assume that the employee has
committed an offence". You should not assume that a person
may not want to learn. If they have difficulty with something new they may simply have a blind spot there. Or there
may be a problem with the way in which it is taught. But
also look back to Question 19 in Skill No. 6.

As for the last item, if there is a disruptive team member
this can be a real problem. If it is unacceptable you may
need to see the book dealing with that topic.

4. Here are the Practical Leadership Skills for comparison:

1.	Maintain or enhance the self-esteem of the employee.
2.	Don't attack the person, FOCUS ON THE PROBLEM.
3.	Don't assume that the employee has committed an offence.
4.	Encourage the employee to express their opinions and make suggestions.
5.	Allow the employee adequate time to think through the problem and to suggest a solution.
6.	Ensure that the employee has an appropriate action programme.
7.	Always set a specific follow-up date.

Please consider which of these skills are reflected in the team leader's fourth checklist below, and mark them off.

SHARING responsibility with the team, welding them together, recognising and using their differences. Therefore:	Which of the seven Practical Leadership Skills?						
	1	2	3	4	5	6	7
Use individuals' skills for the good of the team.							
Use a person with a special skill to develop others. Encourage people to draw on others for help.							
Discuss objectives with the team, ensuring they are realistic.							
Delegate as much as you can, with adequate direction.							
Instil pride: in the organisation, in the team, and in a job well done.							
Show you are on their side - in the right things.							
Encourage the team to meet outside work as well as inside.							
Share good news and bad news.							
Guard against your team becoming insular.							

Comments are on the next page.

Comments

4. Sharing responsibility - without abdicating it - is what every successful team leader needs to be able to do.

SHARING responsibility with the team, welding them together, recognising and using their differences. Therefore:	Which of the seven Practical Leadership Skills?						
	1	2	3	4	5	6	7
Use individuals' skills for the good of the team.	●						
Use a person with a special skill to develop others. Encourage people to draw on others for help.	●						
Discuss objectives with the team, ensuring they are realistic.	●	●	●	●	●	●	●
Delegate as much as you can, with adequate direction.	●	●	●	●	●	●	●
Instil pride: in the organisation, in the team, and in a job well done.	●						
Show you are on their side - in the right things.	●					●	●
Encourage the team to meet outside work as well as inside.	●						
Share good news and bad news.	●	●	●	●	●	●	●
Guard against your team becoming insular.	●		●				

Being part of a successful, high performing team is clearly good for a member's self-esteem; a tremendous motivator.

Ensuring that *you* share with them enables them to share with you, and with all the other members of the team. It is a constant part of your work to maintain balance in all aspects of teamwork - and it requires constant vigilance.

Look after your people and they'll look after you.

MEMBERS' RESPONSIBILITIES

You, as a *member*, but not the leader, of several other teams at work (and perhaps outside work as well) share responsibility for their success and can contribute the same Practical Leadership Skills to the working of those teams - thus playing a full part in the team's achievements.

Most of the paragraph above could be addressed to each of your employees as members of your team and other teams.

The skills can be used as follows.

1. **Maintain or enhance the self-esteem of the employee.**

   ○ Recognise the skills and contribution of colleagues - acknowledge these skills to them and to other members of the team. Help them when necessary.

   ○ Don't be afraid to question anything which seems unfair; you'll probably find that you are speaking for other team members as well.

2. **Don't attack the person, focus on the problem.**

   ○ If people are sometimes slow to grasp problems or put forward ideas, be patient.

   ○ Where there is a misunderstanding you can help by restating the problem in a different way. If a problem is badly defined help to define it clearly.

3. **Don't assume that the employee has committed an offence.**

   ○ Wrong assumptions among one team about another can easily occur. If people let you down don't assume they have done so wilfully. Be open and factual with them about your concerns.

   ○ Don't harbour grudges; most people come to work to do a good job.

Members' responsibilities (Continued)

4. **Encourage the employee to express their opinions and make suggestions.**

   ○ Listen actively.

   ○ Avoid negative body language.

   ○ Support opinions you agree with and seek to build on good ideas.

   ○ Ask questions that clarify without attacking.

   ○ Don't monopolise the discussion.

5. **Allow the employee adequate time to think through the problem and to suggest a solution.**

   ○ If you are always the quickest with ideas others may tend to wait for you to speak first, so be prepared to wait for others to make suggestions. You will get credit for clarifying and supporting those ideas, and for building on them. And the team will benefit too.

6. **Ensure that the employee has an appropriate action programme.**

   ○ If you see something is unclear, or some action isn't allocated then speak up, or ask a clarifiying question.

   ○ Do your share of the work.

7. **Always set a specific follow-up date.**

   ○ Don't allow plans to go unfinished, speak up.

   ○ And, when the follow-up date comes along, be prepared to ask what can be learned from what has led up to it.

> For ideas to be accepted they need to be communicated well - and the boss has limited time. Coaching tools available in the book "Credit where it's due" will help to progress ideas.

So the seven Practical Leadership Skills work both ways - and they provide a convenient shorthand for communication.

MEMBERS' ROLES WITHIN TEAMS

In "bringing out what is in them" (see page 12) the manager needs to build on the strengths of individual employees. At the same time a team needs people to fill different roles[2] if the team is to be balanced and effective.

An extreme example of a *lack* of balance is the team made up entirely of creative "ideas" people who won't listen to each other's ideas; as a result they never reach agreement on what to do. Conversely, a team made up solely of reflective, theorising people may have ideas but be short on action; they develop a super plan but cannot move it forward.

Several team roles have been identified and a team may fail if a key role is not filled. So, when recruiting, the manager wants to know if he needs, eg, an "ideas" person or someone who is better at "finishing", or another type.

This does *not* mean that you have to have a separate person for each role; people may test out as "preferring" a particular role but have the skills for several roles. You may not be able to give them their preferred role - but people can adapt.

Realistically, you may have little control over the balance of your team, having inherited all of them. But if the concept of team roles is not understood, and if the team is not balanced, you could have problems.

As the leader you, of course, exercise control over how the team works.[3] If you use the seven skills in this framework you will, almost certainly, be doing your best in the "here and now" discussions that help the team to work well together and to fill the necessary roles.

So, when you are working with two or more employees think of "*each* employee" rather than "*the* employee" in the framework of seven Practical Leadership Skills.

---

[2] R. M. Belbin, in "Management Teams, why they succeed or fail", Butterworth-Heinemann, 1991, identified several roles. Other writers may describe similar roles but give them different names. Learning styles can be used to describe team roles. See also "Team Management", 1995, Charles Margerison and Dick McCann, published by Management Books 2000.

[3] See "Spectacular Teamwork" by Blake, Mouton and Allen, published 1987 by John Wiley Inc.

Notes

SUMMARY

It has been said that there is nothing so practical as a good theory. So it must be useful to have a way of converting really good theory (in fact several good theories) into action. Accordingly, and it comes as no surprise, the framework of seven Practical Leadership Skills described in this book comes highly recommended.

Practical Leadership Skills

(The all-the-time skills)

1. Maintain or enhance the self-esteem of the employee.
2. Don't attack the person, **focus on the problem**.
3. Don't assume that the employee has committed an offence.
4. Encourage the employee to express their opinions and make suggestions.
5. Allow the employee adequate time to think through the problem and to suggest a solution.
6. Ensure that the employee has an appropriate action programme.
7. Always set a specific follow-up date.

These seven skills offer a well-balanced approach to building effective working relationships between a manager and each employee, between a manager and their whole team and between team members. You can *see* managers using these skills - or not using them.

They help to clarify what the team (large or small) is doing, they help the team advance towards its goals, to recognise that every team member has a part to play, and they help to share responsibility for team achievements - without taking accountability from the team leader.

If you now ever have a discussion that seems unsatisfactory in some way you will probably find that you omitted one or more of these skills, or actually contradicted them. They are not second nature, they have to be worked at - constantly.

There are two more things.

On the right side of the table below are the numbers of those pages where you have made outline action plans. Will you now please scan the previous sections and go firm on the things that you intend to put into practice. List the numbers of the pages and questions/responses.

Practical Leadership Skills

	The Skill	Your action summary
1	Maintain or enhance the self-esteem of the employee.	(Page 27)
2.	Don't attack the person, FOCUS ON THE PROBLEM.	(Page 43)
3.	Don't assume that the employee has committed an offence.	(Page 56)
4.	Encourage the employee to express their opinions and make suggestions.	(Page 73)
5.	Allow the employee adequate time to think through the problem and to suggest a solution.	(Page 86)
6.	Ensure that the employee has an appropriate action programme.	(Page 99)
7.	Always set a specific follow-up date.	(Page 117)

There's now just one more thing.

FINALLY

What about setting a specific follow-up date? To see how you are progressing against your plan? Then another date to check on completion - and to review in order to improve?

A REMINDER?

The framework is reproduced below so that you can, if you wish, have a small card to keep in your pocket or briefcase.

**PRACTICAL
LEADERSHIP SKILLS**

1. Maintain or enhance the self-esteem of the employee.

2. Don't attack the person, **focus on the problem.**

3. Don't assume that the employee has committed an offence.

4. Encourage the employee to express their opinions and make suggestions.

5. Allow the employee adequate time to think through the problem and to suggest a solution.

6. Ensure that the employee has an appropriate ACTION programme.

7. Always set a specific follow-up date.

WORKING TOWARDS A QUALIFICATION?

This book, and others in the series, will help you gain the N.V.Q. unit in Managing People. As it deals only with interpersonal skills it may not match all the elements in that unit. However, these skills can only be used well if supported by knowledge of policies, procedures, your products and services, standards of service, levels of authority, etc. The questions and exercises in these modules ask you to work on these subjects and to take action where appropriate.

ASSESSMENT

For the assessor to decide if you meet the criteria for the NVQ unit on "Managing People" you may:

- be asked questions on all the topics in the unit,

- be asked to simulate interactions with employees, eg, changing unacceptable performance, handling a complaining employee, etc.

The other books in this series will help with specific interactions.

Good luck!